FINAL MISSION
HEROIN TO HERO

PAUL BOGGIE

From Heroin to hero, I saved myself.

"When first hearing of a man's journey from beating Heroin addiction to guarding our late Queen at Buckingham palace, I thought it was a complete fabrication of nice Hollywood style story. But when I see that in fact it was true I had to meet the man himself, Paul Boggie, who is living proof that anything is possible when not only do we put our minds to it, but add a little heart and you will achieve unbelievable things in your life. After bringing his story to life to the stage, what happens next is anyone's guess, but knowing Paul's mind and heart, that red carpet and Hollywood ending is not too far away. But from all this, more importantly I can now call him a friend."

Tony McGeever, Actor and producer, Edinburgh Fringe play "Heroin to Hero"

BOOK DEDICATION

Just a few of the amazing reviews of my first book written on Amazon. It was my first book and took me almost fourteen years to publish. I have learnt a lot since then. A massive thank you for the 379 reviews on Amazon just for the book alone. Let's not forget the hundreds more on my facebook page, **Paul Boggie Author,** please follow me and my journey.

Reviewed in the United Kingdom
"This is without doubt the most honest book that I have ever read, so much so that it's the only book I have ever read twice. Paul Boggie is a true inspiration laying his whole life out for the world to read about. Paul has done everything himself to produce this book and to keep the costs down so that all the profits go to helping homelessness in Scotland. No middlemen profit from this book, all the profits go directly to the people who need it. I found that it helps myself, my wife and wider family members. It doesn't matter what your background is, you WILL take away something useful from this book. In total I've bought four copies and I have given a couple to people I think could benefit from reading it. There is also an audiobook version of this book which I have also purchased from Amazon and if you purchase it you will be surprised by the narrators who read each chapter individually. I'm not going to give anything away about the book or audio book, so no spoiler alerts. Buy a copy today you won't regret it and you will be helping to eradicate homelessness in Scotland."
Dave Walker, Scotland

Proud parents - Reviewed in the United Kingdom on 14 June 2020
"So proud of what you have achieved in your journey and the book just says it all. You have worked so hard son to get where you are today and your Dad and I couldn't be prouder parents. It may have taken 14 years to write but well worth the wait. An author in the Boggie family, so proud of you!"
Lynn and Ian Boggie

Hard hitting, honest and inspiring - Reviewed in the United Kingdom on 20 November 2020
"This is a book you won't forget in a hurry, Paul's story really hits home, from the lowest depths of heroin addiction and the bleak outlook it brings to having the strength and ability to say enough is enough and pull yourself back from the brink, get fit and healthy and achieve a dream of joining the Scots guards, now Paul campaigns to end homelessness in Scotland and raise awareness of addiction, truly inspiring!"

Straight from the heart - Reviewed in Australia on 24 July 2021
"Paul provides a frank and honest account of his journey battling his drug addiction. He is truthful about some of the unsavoury activities he engaged in along the way, but what really comes across is his huge heart and his reflective capacity. It's a story of hope and courage and will surely help others battling their own demons."

Was hooked after the first page - Reviewed in the United States on 31 January 2022
"This inspiring story will motivate anyone who thinks the impossible cannot be achieved. An honest, gripping, account written by a man who overcame the hold heroin had on his life. Not mincing words, Paul Boggie details his years of struggles with heroin in authentic and no-hold-barred writing. his years of struggles with heroin, how his life was controlled by drug addiction, and how he overcame that demon. An authentic story written from his heart, with all the rawness described with honest emotions. He has accomplished his goal to help and inspire others, especially those who are suffering. His aim to raise money for homelessness in his country of Scotland by donating the profits from his book is admirable, Although I found the writing to skip around a lot, the story and emotions that come through make up for it. I also learned a lot of Scottish words I didn't know. I recommend this book for an eye-opener into what it's like to struggle with drug addiction and the ability to conquer it and find happiness."

Powerful - Reviewed in the United Kingdom on 29 August 2022
"Heroin to Hero is real, the message delivered gives everyone a better understanding of addiction, and also gives hope. I was fortunate enough to see the play at the Edinburgh fringe, it gave me goosebumps, tears and humour all in the space of one hour. Paul is inspirational and huge congratulations to the team behind the play, and wish Paul every success moving forward."

A note from Paul Boggie, Author of *Heroin to Hero*
"I am truly thankful to every person who has read my book and left amazing reviews. To my critics, I take on board your feedback - every day is a learning day for me. I am extremely proud to shout from the rooftops that I am clean.

Not every author in this country has donated £13,000 to homelessness charities, for that I am extremely proud."

FOREWORD

Hello, my name is Paul Boggie.

An ex-addict of heroin and prescribed medications, and proud Scots Guardsman, now veteran, serving sentry duties to the late HM The Queen.

I am the proud author of my first self-published book, Heroin To Hero, which sold in excess of one thousand five hundred copies and raised just over £13,500 for which all profits were donated to homelessness in Scotland

I have decided to write this second book as a continuation of the first, in the hope that it can further inspire people. I realised after publishing the first book that there was so much more I wanted to say.

I still believe I can really help people to change their lives for the better. I learned about my mind, applied it to my addiction and mental health challenges and was able to turn my life around.

I really feel a strong urge to share my story so that others can perhaps follow suit. I know and believe you have the ability to change your life around.

I have really enjoyed writing both books and it makes me feel extremely proud to open up my life in such a personal way. At times, it has been raw to recall my past, but I know every time I share, I am strengthening my own focus for today and the future.

I hope that my past sufferings and experiences can be put to good use and I really hope you enjoy reading my story.

My hope is that every page can relate to you in some way and support you with shaping your own goals for each day. Maybe this book will inspire you to support other people in a way you'd not thought about before?

There's laughter, giggles, tears and reflections in my story. I hope the words jump off the page and reach your mind.

I would like to thank everyone for buying the first book because I am truly humbled by the support I have received in trying to raise awareness of addiction issues and this book will hopefully help.

Whether you have suffered with addiction issues or not I think you will enjoy reading my story.

DEDICATION

For my wife and best friend, Steph, you're my rock. Thanks for taking every step with me.

To my daughter Danielle, I hope I make you proud. That's my goal every single day, for you to be proud of me.

My step-daughter Cherise, you're one in a million, our cement.

How can I put into words the unconditional love from my Mum & Dad? You're amazing.

Massive thanks to the amazing talented actor, Tony Mcgeever and the production team for seeing the worth in my story being told on stage. I have made a new life-long friend.

Thanks to Army At The Fringe for offering their venue completely free of charge.

Finally, thanks to the amazing coach Hayley Tennant. She bought my first book and came to see the show at Edinburgh Fringe with her family. Hayley is editor, proof-reader and friend in helping me publish this book.

CONTENTS

1	A Dream Achieved	Pg15
2	Boxing Event	Pg29
3	Gypsy Boxers	Pg33
4	Feature Film	Pg37
5	Drugs	Pg39
6	Married Life	Pg41
7	The Fringe	Pg50
8	Memories of Basic Training	Pg55
9	Crowdfunding and Charities	Pg64
10	Drugs and Stigma	Pg66
11	Feeling Like a King	Pg74
12	Literally Shitting Myself	Pg76
13	School Visits	Pg81
14	Hope and Inspiration	Pg85
15	Homeless	Pg89
16	Living in Fife	Pg93
17	Self-Help	Pg97
18	Growing	Pg101
19	Self-Belief	Pg104
20	Backache	Pg107
21	Writing	Pg115
22	Methadone Programme	Pg117
23	Bullying	Pg119
24	Social Media	Pg121
25	Music	Pg123
26	Peer Support	Pg125
27	Something Missing	Pg126
28	Meadowbank Stadium	Pg128
29	Fireworks	Pg134
30	T in the Park	Pg138
31	Chasing the Dragon	Pg141
32	Courier	Pg143
33	Fringe in Person	Pg145
34	Edinburgh Fringe	Pg151
35	Living in Fear	Pg157
36	Failed Investments	Pg162
37	Society Anger	Pg167
38	Dick Dynamite	Pg169
39	Reflections	Pg172
40	Final Mission	Pg174
41	Goodbye	Pg176

A DREAM ACHIEVED

Since finishing the first book, my life has been yet another high-speed roller coaster. I was addicted to all of my prescription medication when I wrote my last book, and it was a dream to be drug free.

I never put the same pressure on myself as when I broke my heroin addiction 18 years ago. Because of my crushed spine I now had a physical ailment to deal with. The doctors, surgeons and spinal specialists all advised me to accept that a life on drugs was going to be my reality. I believed them full heartedly, so to suddenly have this great idea of stopping was a big deal!

I had sadly become an addict again but whilst I was writing the first book, I was re-educating myself about the power of my mind. If I could apply all I know then I had a chance, but ultimately, the physical excruciating pain would be my biggest barrier and not my mindset.

I started to reduce my prescription medication immediately, and very quickly I was down to half of what I was prescribed by my doctor in only two days. I was still smoking cannabis and decided to leave that addiction until last. I was experiencing some pretty severe pains in my gut, head and chest, and knew it was linked to the copious amounts of tablets I swallowed everyday.

From the day I broke my back I was on codeine, tramadol, gabapentin, pregabalin, amitriptyline and nortriptyline. I never felt any withdrawal symptoms in halving them so I was happy and proud with myself for at least getting to that point. Also, the pain in my back was no different. The hardest stage was going to be experiencing the horrific cold turkey, and I was so anxious to get it over with, so I threw myself wholeheartedly into it.

I decided to snap all my tablets in two and space them out even more.
I remember really struggling more at night so decided to take bigger doses later in the evening. Every single day, when opening my eyes drugs were always on my mind. Self talk was my saviour in these early days of breaking this addiction, "I can achieve this' ', "I will achieve this", as my phrase of choice to myself.

The physical withdrawals never actually got as severe as I was expecting, but mentally it was really tough. I've never been a very good sleeper but I remember being up until early hours of the morning playing my Xbox to distract me. It worked a treat to be honest. Halo Wars 2 is my game of choice, it's a strategy game and requires me to use my brain. When it comes to breaking addictions it's important to find something else to be addicted to, for me it was my Xbox. My thoughts now are, as long as it's not bad for your health then you're definitely onto a winner.

Since coming off heroin eighteen years ago I became addicted to running. I used to run like Forrest Gump all over Edinburgh. As a result my fitness and general health really recovered.

I remember getting down to two tablets and thinking I'd be given these for a sore head.

I decided to just stop taking them and to my surprise, shock and horror my back pain was no worse. I instantly remember feeling happy but very quickly followed by anger!! Imagine if I had tried this nine years ago when I broke my back? Again I would need to find something positive to be addicted to. Running was no longer going to be an option.

Why did I believe the doctors? My life has had enough bitterness and anger to last an eternity so I chose to not let it affect me for long. It would only hurt me and my recovery, so I chose to be proud of myself instead. Opiates are a difficult drug to conquer but there are ways we can help ourselves. Cannabis was my next hurdle. Was this drug the reason my back isn't as bad? I asked myself, I suppose there's only one way to find out. I started putting half the amount into my cigarettes or joints as I call them. I noticed no difference in the way I felt or my back pain at all. I quickly wanted to find out about how easily I could break this addiction and become drug free again. Now this is when I became really excited. Could I achieve something amazing again?

A friend had mentioned that you can get legal cannabis online so I ordered some and started to taper off and replace with the CBD cannabis; I didn't get high so it felt pretty pointless to be spending all that money on it. Cold turkey was the only way to truly find out how my back would cope. After a couple of weeks, I had finished my last joint and had many sleepless nights. To my delight, though my back was no worse, I had become drug free!

This was a dream I never thought I'd ever accomplish in my life! I started to get clarity on my mission in life. Helping the homeless and helping addicts is something that I can do, so I focused all my mind into raising awareness of my book. Which is where my journey on social media began. I promise I could write a book just about the experience I've had on social media but I'll try and filter it down for you.

Social media ... well what can I say? I almost closed my account prior to writing the first book as it really is Fakebook isn't it? I'm fine with people being untruthful but the bullying, cruelty and nastiness is something that affected me in ways that I thought it wouldn't!

After finishing the book I realised that I'd need social media more than ever to raise awareness of what I wanted to and continue to achieve. I began adding strangers on my Facebook page, I opened an Instagram account and also Twitter which was apparently where the celebrities hang out. I found that to be false but I won't go into that too much just now. I was a complete "nobody" to the world so it was going to be a mission.

I was still struggling with my addiction and didn't look healthy either, but in my mind it was clear what needed to be done. Like when writing the first book I realised that I had to be honest, sometimes brutally so. I started to speak about my life story on Facebook and I was extremely nervous, I hated the way I looked and it's a strange feeling hearing your own voice.

The drugs had really taken their toll on my looks and me overall, and I found it really difficult to watch myself back on video. I dug deep and my voice in my head kept saying, "It wasn't about me it was about helping", so I decided to continue regardless. Although I don't like the sound of my own voice, I agreed with what I was saying.

I'm a passionate man and that seemed to come across at least. I've recently ventured onto Tik-Tok too and have over 10,000 followers. I call Tik-Tok "Land of the Trolls'" because there is so much bullying going on! However, there are many lovely people too and I sell books, so it's a good useful tool for me to share my message with people.

I suppose that's why I'm on social media, to raise my profile and make people aware of who I am and what I'm all about. If I can inspire people with my experiences and journey along the way, then it's a massive bonus. During lockdown social media has been essential to sharing my story and promoting my first book, but it has come at a cost to my own mental health at times. I've realised that having an expectation of people is setting myself up for stress. I expected everyone to buy my first book; quite frankly most didn't bother to be brutally honest, including my family which broke my heart a wee bit. My close family did but I have a huge family. My first six months on social media was a complete let down as nobody seemed at all interested in listening to me, I can go on a bit mind you!! Too funny!

Jealousy is probably the reason most tuned out though. Some people hate to see other people getting on in life for the simple reason that they can't, I pity them to be honest. I wish they realised that they can change their whole lives too regardless of where they are at in life. I voice my opinions on my Facebook page and people will say, "stop being negative".

I don't see it that way at all, I just see it as me speaking my truth. I see it as sharing my experience, my reality and how I chose to make a difference with moving away from drugs, from heroin.

Heroin.

That is a word people most dislike to use. It always has a reaction whenever it's mentioned and understandably a negative one. Even when mentioned about getting clean there is a sense of dishonesty. Heroin addicts do lie and many are in denial.

However, you need to show people. Early on when I did my first social media videos I would forgive people for thinking I was still using drugs. It takes a long time to physically recover. I looked like death warmed up and it was clear to see. I knew if I stayed clean I would start to look better. It took about a year, which seems like a long time. It's very gradual but thanks to Facebook I can see my older videos and it shocks me so much. Mentally, I'm the same person with the same drive but I look like a totally different person now.

Social media is great, offering free tools which allows me to share my story around the world. It also gives me the opportunity to reach out to celebrities to ask for help in raising awareness of my book. I decided to start messaging every Scottish actor and singer that I could think of including Facebook, Instagram and Twitter. I targeted everyone that I could think of, so began directly messaging and emailing. I'd take a guess that I sent over five hundred messages, and at the time I totally believed I'd get a reply!

I now know how naive that was but it was good fun trying! When I didn't receive responses from anyone in Scotland, I became a bit deflated with my bubble bursting and felt let down. No way was I giving up though, someone somewhere would see the worth in sharing my story, so I started with the rest of the UK and then the world! In for a penny, in for a pound as they say! If I had listened to them or watched them growing up then I messaged them.

I've decided I won't write any names down for fear of legal action, but trust me, you will all belly laugh when you hear who I was asking for help from! No surprise though to not get a reply and I quickly understood that this was my story and I had to go it alone to ensure my story was told. Every time I was watching tv or listening to music, I would go on my phone and ask for help to promote my book. My first breakthrough came when I was listening to Youtube and a song came on about a guy singing about Easter Road. I'm a big Hibernian fan and I stayed a stone's throw away from the stadium.

I loved the song and he reminded me of Kelly Jones from Stereophonics, another brilliant band I listened to growing up. I clicked his name and another song came on called Salamander Street, too funny, that's in Leith I remember thinking to myself! Who is this guy?
So of course, I immediately went onto social media and tried to reach out to him. A week or so later, I was on Facebook and I got a notification that Callum Beattie was

live, so I joined and watched for a bit. He had over five hundred people watching him and I dropped in a comment saying, "mon the Hibs" which just means, "come on the Hibernian". He read it out to his dad and said my name...properly, pronouncing it perfectly. I ran up the stairs at 1am and woke my wife up to tell her I got a shout out haha!! She wasn't best pleased. I'd woke her up for that, but the following day she said, "well done". I messaged Callum again to say thanks and to my absolute shock got a reply, he knew about my book!

I noticed he had done some work to help the homeless and that's probably why he was giving me the time of day. The next time I was on his live feed on facebook, I just commented "hello", and he saw it! He proceeded to talk about me and my book and I couldn't believe it!

Yes it was the early hours, and yes I ran up the stairs and woke my wife Steph up again! This time she did say "that's an amazing babe", then quickly went back to sleep.
I wasn't sleeping with all the excitement. A few weeks later I was in one of his music videos, just a short clip of me with my book but it meant the world to me and still does. More recently I made a short film with Johnny Brooks and he viewed it and put a big write up on his page. That made me very emotional. Exactly when I needed the support and boost of confidence he was right there publicly supporting me. The boy is an absolute legend in my eyes, turns out he is a Rangers supporter but he can do no wrong haha! As much as I try to be a beacon of light for the addicts of this world he was and still is my beacon of light. Bonus that he sings amazingly and better than Kelly Jones, whom I also love!!

A Facebook friend asked me if I knew a guy called Colin Lillie. I didn't, but she mentioned he was a singer who lived in Australia but he was Scottish. They knew each other and said I should maybe try to reach out to him to help with a charity single I'm putting together. Of course I jumped on social media and had a look. I was sent a Youtube video from my friend which had Colin performing on The Voice Australia. He started to sing and I was instantly hooked, the judges turned and to my shock I recognised one of them, the one and only Boy George!

An internationally known DJ, and most of us know him from "Culture Club".

Colin is also in recovery, as is Boy George and Colin ends up picking him as his mentor. I sent Colin a message to say how amazing I thought he was and to my surprise I got a message back. We organised a zoom call and quickly became friends! We Regularly zoom even up to the present day. He has helped me so much and we are writing a song together for the homeless people. Just like Callum Beattie, I'll never be able to thank Colin enough for all his support. The world of social media was starting to pay off and it made me feel happy that my determination and tenacity was paying off too.

I have been messaging hundreds of people and it was apparent that most won't reply but I won't give up trying. Leo Gregory was a legend who did reply though. I'd been given his Instagram account by a mutual friend and when I messaged him he replied within five minutes or so. I'd grown up watching him on the big screen so you can only imagine my delight when he replied! If you don't know who Leo Gregory is, look him up on Google! At first it was just a fist pump emoji, then I told him I was planning on making a feature film, his reply was one I was certainly not expecting.

I've just looked on my phone to find his reply, and this was the exact message,

"I'd be honoured to pal. Play you, a gangster or someone who's sick on the brown (heroin) whatever you want mate. Of course these things will come down to funding but I believe I will get offers"

It's a very strange feeling to be messaging someone you only know from the television. To date he hasn't publicly supported me. This prevents me from getting too excited to be honest. Still a nice feeling to be responded to. Most have ignored me but I'm not going to mention those people. Life is a learning curve. Everyday is a school day. Perhaps one day Leo will publicly support me but I understand why most don't. That word Heroin! On speaking with people in the celebrity industry I was given a few reasons why celebrities won't support me. First one is snobbery, second one is fear, fear that if they support a book with heroin in the title the media will pick up on it and imply the celebrity has had or has issues with heroin use. Finally, the reason was financial. If they can't make money the agents won't allow it. This makes me angry and sad but there is nothing I can do so I wont be dwelling on it. I actually do understand all the reasons but that doesn't mean I need to agree with them.

There are a few people who have been supporting me on social media that I want to mention in my book. Just to show appreciation. First up is Motorbike Milly. His name is Paul too and his page is all about travelling around on a motorbike with his dog Milly. He was actually the first person with a verified account to comment on my page.

Eddie Kidd OBE, Trevor Coult MC, Stephanine Aird and the boys at Loquacious Live have all supported me publicly too. Guaranteed I will have forgotten to mention someone. They will probably feel a little bit hurt and I can only apologise. I do genuinely appreciate everyone who has helped me raise awareness of my story.

Stay true to myself and in time I will get supported.

Wayne Lineker who is the brother of England footballer Gary has shared my story on Instagram. He actually messages me and supports the homeless too. He owns Ocean Beach in Ibiza. One day I will head over to meet him. As a result of Wayne sharing my story I also had Calum Best share my story on his Instagram. Calum is the son of the late George Best. Calum also replies to me on Instagram. They're a couple of legends in my eyes.

Danny Swanson was another legend who has shown me support in the last year. I remember right back at the start he replied to me and I went on Facebook live saying a Hibernian player had replied to me, little did I know he had moved to St Johnstone haha! Oops, it doesn't matter though he still offered me support, and still does to this day I'm sure we will meet for a cuppa soon!

Chris Small, who I have known my whole life, has agreed to help me with a snooker tournament for charity. Chris is a retired professional snooker player who played at the "State in Leith" In fact, the same club as to where my dad played, and where we learned how to play ourselves. There wasn't much learning in playing snooker in the early days as a young boy, me and my brothers were there to pick the coloured balls out the pockets and repost them as my dad knocked century after century. I absolutely hated it!

When my dad messed up I grabbed my chair and moved it to where the white ball was, clamber up on the chair, take my shot and miss. Yep, back to picking the balls out the pockets again. Chris had his own table which I had the privilege of playing on one occasion. Chris was just like my dad though, just looking for someone to pick the balls out of the pockets. Sadly, he retired due to spinal problems but not before he beat John Higgins and Ronnie O' Sullivan to go on and win the LG cup in 2002. What an absolute legend!

My dad has an amazing amount of trophies for football, golf and snooker and out of the three sports, I'd probably say I could have progressed at snooker the most.
I used to practise at the State before it was closed and then I moved to the Ballroom at Jocks Lodge. Like golf it was a sport I could play on my own and I liked that. I played for the Leith team years ago but wasn't accomplished enough and my bottle and nerve always crashed. In practice, I could knock them in easily but with an audience I always got flustered.I grew up with a cue, golf club and football in my hand but never committed enough to learning.

I have regrets about not being committed to the stuff I loved, my life had other plans.

Back to social media. Another great musician who messaged me out the blue was Billy Lockett. I love his music and he's great on the piano too. He was just congratulating me on the book. Another legend who had the decency to reply to his fans. Apparently, all these celebrities have not seen my messages so I won't bad mouth anyone haha! It has caused me much frustration over the years but I was never giving up. My thought process was that surely these celebs care about the homeless as much as me and although I had been a heroin addict in my life, I showed true determination to turn it around and I thought being a Guardsman, serving century duties to HM The Queen, would aid in my plea for help.

On another note, truth be told, I was expecting more support from the army than I received, but there are some gems who support me in the army. If I was still serving as an elite ScotsGuard, then I'd easily get an audience with celebs to help me. I loved my time in the army so I could never say anything bad, just disappointment I suppose. Even the military charities refused to help with my book, "conflict of interest" I was told.

Conflict of interest? For what exactly? Here I am a veteran, a previous serving member of the army, part of an elite division serving HM The Queen - to be told, "a conflict of interest".

Sometimes my mind really does boggle.

I suppose my expectations from people and organisations is what got me upset, I soon realised that my story was what it's all about. I decided to fly solo regardless and I was determined to not let it get to me too much. My voice, my book and my story will help people so I can sleep easy at night knowing that. It would have been nice though for more legends to acknowledge my reach, my communications to them. I will never understand ignorance.

I set up a support group on Facebook and began sharing my story and thoughts on breaking addiction. If I can help just one person then it's all a worthwhile cause for me.

I have helped people that I know of and probably many more that I don't.

Planting seeds in people's minds is what I do. That's how I broke my heroin addiction almost seventeen years ago. Someone planted a seed at the possibility of change. I believe from my experience that the hardest people to get to realise their potential are addicts, so I definitely have my work cut out for me. I won't mention too much more about the support group because it was and remains confidential but I can tell you that I have helped people become opiate free. Staying that way is always the battle we face and my only hope is that they can achieve it like I did. I am extremely proud of myself.

I have eighteen thousand followers on my social media to date and ten thousand of those are on Tik-Tok, "Land of theTrolls" haha! Too many bullies and nasty people on that app!!

I've been banned from doing live videos because I kept mentioning the title of my book! I hope to get back on soon as I was selling copies everyday when I went live. I can also play music which is something I can't do on Facebook. The police on Facebook are forever shutting my videos down or muting them as I don't have or own the copyright. I bet Callum, Colin and Billy didn't mind though. Maybe I should ask them?

One thing that social media has really helped me with is telling my story with podcasts.

I never knew what a podcast was until my journey on social media began. It's basically an interview, an outlet for people to talk in audio format. A host would ask me questions and it allowed me to share my story worldwide. America, India and all across the UK people have helped me share my story, pretty amazing when you think about it!

One guy that I must mention is a crazy American called Arron, from Ohio USA. He had invited me to do a podcast and we quickly hit it off, what a great laugh he is, very charismatic. He too is in recovery and he really seemed to appreciate me and my story so we stayed in touch and are still good friends today. We occasionally do live videos together. "Across the pond" we call it, and it's basically just two guys having a laugh. Colin joined us too and we call that across the world because Colin is in Australia, three guys in recovery that would never have hooked up and became friends if it wasn't for social media.

Like drugs, for every high and up there is a crash-down. The media is absolutely no different. Yes, I've had a lot of support come from unexpected people. Complete strangers choosing to get on board and share my story. I'm not being honest if I don't tell you of the many negatives though. I won't mention anyone's name but a lot of people have become jealous as my journey grows or have looked in and instantly became jealous.

I believe they have chosen to hate me because they can't achieve what I have. All I've ever wanted to do is inspire people to change and I'm proud to say I'm good at it! However, when people are not ready for real change, then it's difficult for them to see how I could actually help them. So many addicts are on my social media and because I don't know these people it's really hard to filter out the genuine from the not so genuine people. I try to give everyone an opportunity to help themselves and guide them through the troubled waters. Addiction is one of the hardest battles to win and not everyone has it in them to fight. So many people that continue to battle just can't open their minds up to the possibility of change of course, my experience is, when they fail it's "all my fault".

Embrace me instead of hating me and perhaps you can change too.

As for the famous or well known people of Scotland then all I can say is, I'm massively disappointed. I've been tweeting, emailing, and messaging since I finished the first book and the vast majority did not respond. Not even a courteous, "thanks but no thanks".

Apparently they probably did not see my messages but I'm not buying that from them at all! They think that I want to make money off their name or just don't care about the homeless or addicts of this country perhaps? It's easy to say you care if you're in the public eye and with media help the public will believe it, however there are so many financial benefits to donating to organisations that I question whether they genuinely care. Just my opinion of course, and I've yet to be proved wrong. Fame and fortune is what it's all about and money is the root of all evil. Greed is in everyone, I believe, just at different levels,

Although I feel let down by so many people I won't let that ever stop me. In fact it just makes me more determined, my whole life people have doubted me and if I had just given up as a result of that then I wouldn't be here writing now. I chose and choose to get on with these things and steer my own course. Being on social media was an unexpected journey but because of the lockdown it was necessary. I don't know if I've always been on social media but I've met some great people so who knows.

Without a publisher or a marketing company to help spread the word of my book I was really left with no choice.

Callum Beattie and me.

My Dad

Eddie Kidd, MBE. An honour to see him with my book

Comedian, Dee Maxwell with my book

My Mum and Dad with my first book

BOXING EVENT

Last June, I organised a charity boxing event, I had some help of course and that came in the hands of Alfred McArthur.

I never knew who Alfie was, but he saw a Facebook live video when I was talking about raising money and he called me directly after.

Alfie is in the Scots Guards and he's also a professional boxer so I was excited he was offering to help. We spoke for hours every night discussing what to do. At first he offered to fight someone and donate the purse to the cause, but as our discussions continued we decided to hold a charity event which consisted of pro-boxers covering one hundred miles in four days.

I asked the pro-boxers on social media but not one replied. I was relying on Alfie to use his contacts to get some names for me. With my injuries I really had to rely on Alfie to do the hundred miles by himself if need be, but fortunately we did get some bodies to take part. As with most things in life there was going to be a financial burden.

I don't have any regrets about using my savings to hold the charity event. I wont say how much money I spent but, I had a great time meeting everyone. It was a once in a lifetime opportunity!

The organising of the event was the most stressful thing ever, I had so many people pulling out in the last week that I found myself tearful and angry a lot of the time. I refused to give up even though most people advised it. I packed the car full of all my kit for the week and I also took a tonne of military clothing for the boxers too. I drove down to the Yorkshire Dales on my own to meet Alfie. He was in the barracks and didnt have too far to travel. I remember arriving and meeting Alfie for the first time. We just looked at each other and laughed. It's going to be hard for them, he said haha!!

I just looked at the rolling hills of the Dales and the great big grey clouds that surrounded us on all sides and said oh well with a big cheesy grin on my face! I would be living with the guys in the wilderness but I wouldn't be taking part in the hundred miles, instead I would follow in the Range Rover with water and supplies and just hope nobody got hurt.

I was really worried about injuries as these guys were professional sports people and a serious injury could affect their careers. We had one night on our own before the boxers arrived so it gave me and Alfie a chance to get acquainted. The first problem we had was where to camp. I let Alfie take control of the decisions and he went off and scouted a spot. When he returned we emptied both vehicles and quickly realised how much kit we had both brought. Please remember that I have a crushed spine and only recently came off my medications so I was extremely anxious. I'm too determined for my own good at times, and did not want Alfie to think I was soft so I gritted my teeth.

We picked up all the kit we could carry and headed to this amazing spot Alfie had picked out, "NO!! Alfie are you kidding me", I bellowed, I was laughing but inside I was horrified. It was a marshland!

Full of fallen trees and branches sticking out the ground, literally not even a clear spot to pitch our two-man tents. We cleared an area as best as we could and set up tents on top of the big branches! It was going to be getting dark soon and we were in the middle of nowhere. The weather was good but rain was forecast so we made sure our kit was waterproof. We made some food and had a cuppa then got our heads down.

Alfie was against lighting a fire which really pissed me off, I lit a small one anyway as the midges were out in force. Light discipline was something from the army and I understood it but I'm not in the army anymore, the only enemy we had was the god damn midges.

There were another two potential enemies we encountered on day one, WILD HORSES!! Now, I know many of you will be thinking horses are harmless, however if you read the first book you'll know that a horse called "Smash" bit me in Canada so I'm always very wary!

They started to show too much interest in us and I hadn't packed any carrots. Alfie was winding me up all day saying that "they were coming for us". You can imagine my shock when they actually did venture into our wee camp, standing, staring and glaring straight at me!! Alfie raucously laughing in the background did not help the situation, not at all!
They spooked very easily and I sat like a statue trying to not look back at them in the eyes as they may see that as a challenge. Eventually they wandered off but this wouldn't be our last encounter,

The following morning Jack and Victor were back (these are the names I gave to the wild horses!). This time they came even closer to us and I was a bit scared to be honest with you. Alfie made a loud noise with a mess tin and they bolted away. I shouted at Alfie as they could have attacked me!! We realised our camp was no good for when the boxers arrived so we decided to pack up and move. We had to cross an open marshland maybe a mile in distance to where we planned to camp. We were halfway there with all of our kit on our backs and guess who decided to show up? Yes Jack and Victor were back and this time they didn't look happy we were approaching their area. I dropped all my bags and prepared to run.

Alfie is a soldier and pro-boxer so I didn't fancy my chances of out-running him. If Jack and Victor charge then they are coming for me. I scanned the area until I saw a tree big enough and planned my escape! They wandered off though to my relief.

Our new camp was much more open and right next to the loch, jaggy nettles everywhere and crows were making an absolute racket but I wasn't moving again; my back was beginning to give way after the short hike so we set up,

I was getting nervous with the thought of meeting the boxers. Ben Jones was an accomplished boxer, Dave Dickenson was a PGA tour golfer, and Paul Rodgers was an olympic runner. They were Ben's friends so I invited them to join us. Johnny Edwards had allowed three gypsy boxers to attend from his boxing club so we would have a good turn out, The gypsy boxers didn't turn up until it was dark later that night. Last but not least was Krispats who is a Latvian boxer, he was travelling with the gypsy boxers so we wouldn't see him until later on that night.

Ben, Dave and Paul were all really friendly and laid back which put me at ease. They all had a cracking sense of humour which was welcomed. They were going to need it!! We gave them military clothing and asked them to change. This was a military style exercise and we played some games with them to help break the ice. Let me tell you, camouflage cream is not easy to come off but we let them plaster it on as I was recording a film! Reception on the phone meant I couldn't go live like planned, so I'd taken lots of little videos to hopefully make a DVD for UK homelessness and the NHS.

Here I am, sixteen years old - with a horse I liked, and it didn't bite me!

GYPSY BOXERS

Geoff Dixon, Peter Nurdin and Shawn Grant were the gypsy boxers and having never really spent time with gypsies in general, I was curious about spending a week with them. They rocked up six hours late but I certainly wasn't saying anything to them; although, Alfie claimed he would until he saw the bloody size of them!!

 These guys were huge and it was clear from early on that they did what they wanted when they wanted. Again, they brought a sense of humour and a willingness to get stuck in so I was over the moon they made it. Geoff talked more than me which is an achievement in itself, Ben was a chatterbox too so i spent most of the week listening Amazing boxing stories were shared and stories of living as a gypsy. As the week went on everyone opened up and we had a brilliant laugh. I was proud of myself for arranging this event and was making some great memories with amazing people who supported my journey to help people.

The following day we set off to start the first twenty five mile mile trek. We had set up a few curve balls for them too and I soon realised how fit these guys were!
Push up challenge and a heavy lift carry were added to the twenty five miles and not once did anyone moan about it. We split the teams up so they would become competitive. I knew from my army days that if you challenge someone they will try harder if they are competing.

 I was a mere cameraman of course, although I did do some push ups. Gypsy boxers were going to add a different dimension to this event and I loved it. After day one we all drove miles to the nearest shop. The gypsy boxers had a white M3 convertible and Geoff was always sitting up in the back seat with a slingshot in hand. Pheasants, rabbits, basically anything that moved got the wrath of the sling from Gypsy Geoff. These guys cooked and ate anything they killed and they have my absolute respect for that. At the shops we all looked like a bunch of squaddies and the general public were intrigued about us.

 At night we lit a fire to Alfies disbelief, and we had a few beers, Dave brought the golf clubs out and we hit golf balls into the loch. It was summertime so it wasn't dark until 10pm. Gypsy boxers often left the camp for hours at a time, I wasn't too sure what they were getting up to, but I later found out they had been flashing to the locals! No surprise there, I found it funny and amusing but I was responsible for these guys!

 Day two and our second twenty five mile trek, spirits were high and the weather started off good but soon turned into torrential rainfall in true Yorkshire Dales fashion. I noticed that nobody was complaining and I was super proud of them all. I actually felt bad that I couldn't take part, my back was playing up but i never brought it up much, I'd recently stopped all my meds too, so struggled a wee bit.

We were supposed to do a loch crossing but for safety reasons I decided against it. I'd settle for everyone getting in the water for a wash. I had a vote on facebook and most people voted for me to go first so I did, the very least I could do after all the hard work the boys put in. Alfie bottled it though, but everyone else jumped in. A true gypsy wash Geoff shouted, as he gathered himself up with soap and proceeded to do push ups under the water, what a guy, what a laugh! Peter and Shawn quickly followed suit. I have a video of course.

The third day and tempers were starting to fray a wee bit, sleeping arrangements weren't great and food was military ration boxes or noodles although we did cook spaghetti bolognese one night. Weather was rubbish and feet were blistering because of the boots. To their credit though, they still went out and achieved the twenty-five miles.they stopped at a waterfall, jumped under it but had no way of drying their feet, so they soldiered on and trench foot began to set in.

I remember looking at Alfie and saying that I was cancelling the event because of the state of the gypsy boxer's feet. We helped them dry their feet and fortunately they did improve. I got such a fright because these guys are pro-boxers and trench foot is no laughing matter.

The final day was the most difficult for me, my back pain was severe and we had to pack up to head home later in the day. The boys headed out to complete the one hundred miles. I was trying to pack up all the kit and felt totally drained and in need of pain relief. I was determined not to use drugs so I just tried my best to get on with it. The guys finished the target walk and helped me pack up the last of our kit, we took some pictures and said goodbye.

Stress had got the better of me and I broke down in tears in the car. I will only say that I spent thousands of pounds to organise this event out of my personal savings and I got a few hundred pounds back. To date no money was made for charity and I'm still thousands in the red, I loved my week with the boys though. The world of social media reared its ugly head again and literally nobody supported me. "Go fund me" seemed a good idea but you need an audience, something I never had, big thanks to everyone who did donate though! I'll put all the unseen footage together and make a dvd or something and raise some money for charity and regain my lost savings too. Marketing companies is something I don't do but this event needed it. Lesson learned and next time I'll know.

Me and the boxers at the charity event I organised.

Our boxing event

Great teamwork!

FEATURE FILM

So after publishing the book I had many messages about making a documentary and feature film. I made a short facebook video and posted it to all the film groups I could find.

I was astounded by how many people responded, filmmakers, actors, film crew and assistant producers too. I set up a zoom meeting with all twenty three of them but only sixtook part. They all told me a film is a great idea and destined for London or even Hollywood!

All I had to do was be patient and the chance will come. From that day I've had my heart set on the big screen. After a few false starts I finally got a production company to help me. That was the day I became less stressed about the lack of support I received. They believe in me and believe in my story more importantly. I'll be forever grateful to them for taking a chance on me. My feature film which was once a mere dream, but now will be a reality and most people will be shocked at my achievement.

My story is unique and amazing regardless of what Facebook thinks, and anyone else for that matter. I had a dream and vision and followed it, even when people were being nasty or laughing at me. My determination ensured I wasn't giving up and I'm actually so very proud of myself.

I've done a couple of short films too which helped me raise awareness. I've been in the Sunday Times, The Sun, Central Fife, Times 4 Times and Edinburgh Live a few times. I've spoken to the Drug Minister of Scotland along with a few other SMPs and more influential people too. I've certainly been putting myself on the map. Of course, I'm far from finished. More people will see what I'm doing and reach out to offer support to me. I want to try to be the creative director in the film so I can ensure my story isn't changed too much. I don't think it needs to be too dramatised to be honest.

Funding is what is needed and I believe I will get it. I don't rule out Hollywood either, you're probably laughing right now haha, and I understand why, but my mind won't allow me to stop believing in myself. I doubt I'd have reached this far if it did. Watch this space folks.

Leo Gregory being in my film is something I'm super excited about, a few others that I can't mention by name too. Who knows I may even play a part, I'm already technically an actor as I played a very small part in the film "Dick Dynamite" which will be released next year.

Don't worry, it's not a porno!! I played a German soldier in the film who is shot in the head. I don't even speak but it was a great day filming and let me see and experience what a film set is like. I'm certainly used to cameras being in my face now so I don't worry about the future.

Thankfully, I look healthier than I did last year at the beginning of lockdown. Beans Goldblum is the man behind "Dick Dynamite" and I came across him through a mutual friend Maximus Mcneil, both great guys. Maximus was Begbies body double in "Trainspotting 2" and also the star of the "Bouncer" on BBC iPlayer with over three million views.

In "Dick Dynamite", anyone with a name like Beans Goldblum is going to be a legend and I wasn't wrong! He is in a rock band and has the biggest head of hair I've ever seen, not that I'm jealous of course! I'll be promoting the film so look out for it late in 2022.

Maximus always says he would be honoured to play me in the film too, but I will hold auditions for that part. It'll be a battle between Leo and Maximus! Scott Collins is another professional actor who would happily play me, he is also a veteran and a great guy. I'm just really honoured that these guys want to be considered to play me!

Here's me playing a German soldier in the film "Dick Dynamite"

DRUGS

It's sad that I'll always be a junkie to some, regardless of what amazing things I do in life. It's difficult at times not to be angry.

 I choose to pity people who judge me in a negative way. My life has had drugs at the centre for most part so I can't blame anyone really. It was my bad choices that ended with me becoming an addict. Nobody forced me to take them so it was all totally self-inflicted. I have become an accomplished motivational speaker and I hope to change peoples' minds about drug addicts. I recently visited my first prison of many to talk about drug issues. I have many more school and prison visits lined up too. It's an honour to be asked to return. The prison has bought twenty four copies of my book for the library.

 That makes me extremely happy and proud. Drugs are here to stay and the sooner society acknowledges this the better. Education is king in this life and people need more education.

 What I have taken from my life is that it was a mind problem that I was challenged with. I had no chance of ever fixing myself without fixing my mind. The course I attended that allowed me to break my heroin addiction had nothing to do with addiction. When people ask me how and can I help them break their addictions I always say fix your mind and everything else will fall into place, not just your addiction issues but all aspects of your life.
One thing that inmates have is time to reflect, so I really hope I can do some good on my visits.

 On the first visit the prison officer who set it all up took me into the area where I'd be doing my talk. I was very nervous if I would be recognised, as I know many people who are in prison. One guy looked at me and instantly said, "I recognise you from somewhere"!! He was from the same area as me but I didn't recognise him and I'm brilliant with faces, perhaps it was my brother? Anyway, we all sat down and I spoke about the book and my battles with addiction. Suddenly the phone in the office rang and Jamie stood up and walked off to answer it!! Where the hell is he going? I was thinking to myself, it was only him there looking after me. He stepped into his office and closed the door.

 I could see through the glass that he had his back to me and my anxiety was clear for all to see. That was a long 5 minutes let me tell you. The guys were all awesome with me though, I started to answer questions that the guys had. The first question was do I believe in destiny?

Quick reply for that one as I definitely do now! They asked if the crash was somehow a sign that I had no place in Afghanistan. One thing we all agreed on is that I have my work cut out for me trying to change people's minds on addicts and convicts, I explained that it won't stop me trying,

Alcohol is the most destructive drug in my opinion and it's legal. Yes, people can enjoy a drink and not become addicted to it but if you are unfortunate enough to, then it destroys lives just like heroin. I've never had a real issue with drinking, I remember in basic training and doing my ceremonial duties in London that I was drinking a lot. Fear of going to Afghanistan was the most likely reason I drank, alongside everyone else who were doing it. I did enjoy it, well the first few pints anyway!

When I moved onto whisky I would be lying if I said I could remember most occasions. Like with drugs I was super greedy on the drink, emotional wreck at times, If I wasn't angry, I would be crying.

Here I am, 18 years old after taking heroin

MARRIED LIFE

The only hero in my life is my wife, who nursed me back to health after my car crash. Twice I've broken serious drug addictions! First time round it was Cyrenians who saved me with the course to do with understanding my mind. I'm eighteen years off heroin. Second time around a soulmate with no experience of drugs picked me up...literally! I remember not being able to walk when I first came out of hospital, moving me from chair to bed every night. Cooking, cleaning and everything that goes with caring for someone, possibly even wiping my arse at times!

I was broken physically and mentally, Steph never once moaned at me.

Trust me when I say I'm a hard person to live with. I never wanted to get married and was vocal about the fact for most of my adult life. Something was definitely different with Steph. A genuine caring and understanding woman showing interest in me so I would have been daft not to get married. To me it's just a bit of paper that means nothing,

True marriage is carried in the heart and mind of the individuals. I think the reason we will make it forever is that when I'm moody and unbearable she knows to leave me to sulk. I am not as bad nowadays, but when I was on my prescribed drugs my moods were all over the place. Leave me alone doesn't mean let's have an argument about why I'm not going to leave you alone!! Steph always leaves me be and I love her dearly for it. I wouldn't be here now doing what I'm doing if she didn't care about me the way she does. I need to vent sometimes, and having someone that will listen and judge was important when I look back, and of course still is today.

We first met at Safeways supermarket where we both worked. I had just started abusing heroin back then and girls were the last thing on my mind. We later hooked up after my car accident and became very close. I truly have my soulmate now and behind every good man is a good woman. I am settled now and extremely lucky. Happiness in relationships is special.

Steph has a daughter Cherise. She was eight when we first started dating. This was the main obstacle for me to overcome. It wasn't the fact that I had an issue looking after someone elses kid, It was more the fact that I failed miserably as a dad before and was worried I'd make the same mistakes and let Cherise down.

Cherise was a little character who quickly had me wrapped around her little finger. I also noticed how much she had her mum wrapped around her little finger too. This caused some arguments early in the relationship. Steph was spoiling her too much and it really annoyed me. I believe kids should earn treats as a good way of teaching them for later in life.

One night I was staying at Steph's parents house on weekend leave from the army. The parents were away at their caravan so we had the house to ourselves. We cooked lasagne and settled down to watch the film Armageddon. Cherise comes through from her bedroom quite late that evening demanding an ice cream. Not one from the freezer either, she wanted one from the shop. I couldn't believe it when Steph got up and put her trainers and jacket on. If it was up to me I would have said have an ice cream from the freezer or go without.

We had a small argument about it a few days later and Steph explained that she felt guilty because she had split from Cherises dad. I totally understood and it helped me understand why she was spoiling Cherise. I stand corrected because at the time I voiced that if you keep spoiling her she will grow up to be a little bitch. This couldn't be further from the truth with Cherise. She had always been well mannered as a child and fortunately she carried it on to the amazing young woman she is now.

We did have a few moments early on. Like the time we were trying to teach her to be more independent. She was only eleven or twelve so we started with the little things. "OK Cherise me and your mum would like a cup of tea please"

She knew how to put the kettle on, which was something at least. As she was holding the cup to pour the water into the cups she spilt some water on her hand and burnt it.

I also did this as a young kid and had to go to hospital.

Fortunately Cherise didn't. It was a little red and swollen and I felt awful. 'Did you purposely do that to get out of making cups of tea all the time?' She denied it of course and we went back to making our own cups of tea for the foreseeable future. I wasn't letting her off the hook too much though. She came through from her bedroom a few weeks later, kicking her leg up in the air like a ballerina as she often did. 'Mum can I have toast please?' Before Steph could answer I told her to make it herself. She just gave me a shocked glance and then looked at her mum.

I asked Steph not to move and if Cherise wanted toast she would have to make it herself. What harm could come to her? I told her to get the bread from the cupboard and guided her from the living room on what to do and more importantly what not to do. She always had Nutella on her toast so I told her she would need a knife from the cutlery drawer. 'Whatever you do, don't ever stick a knife anywhere near that toaster' I told her.

When the toaster pops, that's the toast ready. "Be careful the bread will be hot and we don't want you burning yourself again", Steph shouted. We both chuckled.

Cherise managed to do it all by herself. Even bringing her plate back to put on the kitchen bunker for someone else to wash. Dishes would never be something Cherise would do. I wasn't bothered though neither was Steph. Slowly but surely we were teaching her things about the house and it was going really well.

Steph was always one for buying new kettles and toasters and I never understood why. It wasn't like they did a better job or would make tea and toast taste any different. For a quiet life I let her get on with it. Happy wife, happy life as they say. £120! For a kettle and toaster! 'Are you having a laugh? I asked if the kettle and toaster did any special tricks like make the tea and toast themselves. She got what she wanted and that's all that mattered to me.

The following week Steph was at work and Cherise came in from school demanding toast but this time she wanted cheese on toast. I was reclined on my comfy chair playing the Xbox so I wasn't moving. I told her to do it herself so she went to the kitchen and began making her toast. Next thing I know the fire alarm is sounding and the house is filling with smoke! I jumped up off my comfy chair and ran into the kitchen. I turned the toaster off at the wall socket and grabbed a dish towel and began to wave it about like a madman.

Eventually after opening all the windows and door we got the alarm to go off. I entered the kitchen to see what had happened. This expensive toaster better have a warranty I remember thinking. As I inspected the toaster I noticed the bread hadn't popped up so I put the power back on and tried to sort it.

The reason the bread didn't pop up was because Cherise had taken cheese slices and stuck them to the bread prior to putting them in the toaster. That was a learning curve that day. I don't want to embarrass Cherise too much but I have to tell you about the time we had to vacate the flat in a hurry. I was in my usual spot playing the Xbox. Steph was at work and Cherise came in from school hungry as usual.

I'm a self confessed lazy arse and I wasn't moving. 'Can I make tomato soup please Paul?' I agreed and I had shown her how everything works in the kitchen so I wasn't worried.

I heard her heading into her bedroom so everything must have gone well. If she isn't sure she usually asks so I continued to play my Xbox. I had asked her to close the living room door so she wasn't disturbing me. It was about thirty minutes later I got up to go to the toilet and as I opened the door I was met with a horrific smell of gas. It actually took my breath away. It was that strong I had to squint my eyes. I freaked out and shouted for Cherise to get out of the house in an aggressive manner. The poor bairn had no idea why I was screaming at her as she opened her bedroom door with tomato soup on her lips. 'Run to your grandads' I told her. As we both left in a hurry. I called the gas board because I thought a pipe had burst or something. I was heavily medicated but that sure woke me up in a hurry. As I'm standing in the garden waiting on the gas board I had visions of explosions so ran round all the neighbours doors to get them out too.

After five minutes I started to think what could have caused it. I remember Cherise had asked for tomato soup and could that have something to do with it. I bravely or stupidly ran back upstairs and into the flat with my T-shirt over my face.

I went to the gas cooker and noticed one of the hobs was turned all the way to the max and had not been lit. The gas was bellowing out and I realised she had just turned it the wrong way. Panic was over and teaching kitchen skills with Cherise would need to continue. I had no plans to become less lazy, that's for sure. I told her how lucky we were because I smoked cigarettes and a naked flame could have blown us all up. A little dramatic perhaps but wanted to scare her a wee bit.

I could not have asked for a better stepdaughter and we have become close friends. I think I didn't do too bad a job of bringing her up. Steph tells me I did an amazing job and I suppose that's all that matters.

One final story about Cherise is the problems we would have with her eating habits. She wouldn't eat her tea and it drove me nuts. I stopped all the junk food when she came in from school. No tomato soup, no cheese and toast either. I noticed she was asking for a can of Coca Cola with her tea and she would sit and guzzle it down and pick at her food. Moving it around the plate to try make it look like she had eaten more than she had. I was young once too, I told her. Not born yesterday. I told her that when I was her age I used to go to the toilet and spit the chewy bits of meat into toilet tissue and flush them away. We all had our tricks I suppose. I banned fizzy juice from meals to see if that would help. She was just a fussy eater.

Every weekend when I came home from the army I stood Cherise by her bed. Teaching her how to stand to attention. I ransacked her whole bedroom every weekend searching for contraband. Crisps, Jelly sweets, chocolate or fizzy juice. They are all banned from the bedroom until you start eating your dinner I told her. Steph and Cherise both found it amusing but I was serious.

Steph always supported me when I was a little strict with Cherise. She understood why I was doing it. I didn't want Cherise to grow up having everything handed to her on a plate. I know many little spoiled brats and it's caused by the parents.

All I wanted in life was to settle down and the only way I could do that was to find someone that I could be best friends with. I had a list of things in my mind that I wanted. Someone that isn't selfish. Someone that isn't pretentious. Finally someone that I could have a laugh with. I have a strange sense of humour and don't take things too seriously. Life is too short to be bothering with people like that.

I had to test the waters to find out how Steph would react to my humour. 'Make me a cup of tea ya fanny' I demanded. It was nice to have Steph reply with, "of course I will master and I'll also load it with salt for you". This was to become a regular joke between us amongst other things. Basically, I could be a cheeky shit and Steph wouldn't get offended yet give me it back. After ten years together we are still exactly the same.

We became the best of friends and realised that we liked each other's company so much that we stopped socialising with other friends so much. We were happy sitting in the flat every weekend watching films. People say that spending too much time with someone isn't healthy. I disagree totally. Proof is in the pudding and we hardly ever argue. We belly laugh everyday and I don't take it for granted.

We quickly settled into a life that made us both extremely happy. I knew I had met my soulmate and would do everything I could to hold onto her. Life isnt perfect for any couple and we did have a couple of things to test our strength.

One day I came in and I could tell Steph was worried about something. I asked what was wrong and she didn't answer straight away which made me angry. 'Just spit it out, will you?' I told her. 'I'm pregnant!' she replied. I was totally shocked and didn't know what to say. Eventually I asked how? She replied with 'I'm sure you were there too! We both laughed and started to discuss what we were going to do.

Having more kids wasn't part of the plan for either of us but if I was going to have more kids it would be with Steph. We decided we would be great together and started to get excited. I had my own issues to deal with because I'd already failed once but I was a different person now. I loved Cherise and was doing a good job so I could see myself managing a lot better this time around.

We didn't tell many people and wanted to wait until we went for the scans. I remember thinking that I wanted a boy. We went for one of our scans and I remember sitting on the chair next to Steph as she lay on the hospital bed. They put the jelly on her stomach and I was just watching the health worker's face and not the screen. Something was wrong! The health worker called on another colleague to come over. My heart sank but I was trying to be brave for Steph. Steph was told that she had miscarried and I felt numb. This was going to make us or break us and it was clear how much I had fallen in love with Steph at this point.

I tried to be as supportive as I could. It wasn't meant to be and we had each other. We grew a lot closer after the miscarriage. Time is a great healer as they say. We didn't really discuss it because I didn't want to upset her. We were both heartbroken and it would do neither of us any good to keep bringing it up. If it was a test to see how strong we were as a couple then we passed it.

Steph sadly lost her mum to cancer a few years ago and this was the most difficult thing to deal with. I have never felt so helpless in all my life. I noticed how much she had changed after and there was nothing I could do other than be there. I purposely never really spoke about it because I didn't know what to say. Steph's mum Lorraine liked me and had known me for many years as we worked together in Safeways.

I remember telling Lorraine that I would look after Steph and we were going to get married. 'I know you will son' she told me. That was the last time I spoke with her. I just tried my best to be there and if Steph wanted to talk then I was willing to listen. I still have both my parents so I couldn't relate with how she was feeling hence my feeling of hopelessness.

Steph is my world and I would do anything to ease her pain. When bad things happen it's a test of our relationship and we are stronger than ever as a result. I honestly couldn't have wished for a better partner.

How Steph dealt with me and my demons was and still is amazing.

Never judging me and being completely understanding of my situation. I was in a really dark place after being medically discharged from the army. I tried my best to hide it and of course I had my medications to help me escape my reality. I loved how happy and content I was when we were together. That's all that mattered to me and I had a dream of fixing myself again but reality is I doubt Steph thought I'd achieve it. I never thought I would.
Being on drugs didn't bother Steph too much. She certainly never pressured me to stop. She was concerned about my back and didn't want to see me in pain.

When the time came to stop all my medications and cannabis I think I scared Steph a little bit. The night I finished the first book I had changed forever. A lightbulb moment happened again and I realised the error of my ways. The mind is the most powerful tool and I had unfortunately forgotten. I was very impatient and wanted everything done yesterday.

Steph could easily write a book about those first few months. She never once doubted me or if she did she never voiced it. I knew she would have my back regardless and this really helped. When I was voicing my plans for the future she would just let me vent and get it off my chest.

I'm fully aware of how lucky I am to have Steph and Cherise in my life. They both saved me when I was at a time I needed saving. The reason the darkness left my life was because I had Steph and Cherise bringing me so much light and laughter everyday.

Cherise, aged 8 and me. Cheeky grins!

My beautiful Steph on our wedding day. My rock.

Steph, me and Cherise on her birthday

THE FRINGE

A social media friend Maxumus O'neill who played Begbies body double in "Trainspotting 2" has been helping me promote my story to everyone he comes across. Albeit he was calling me "Paul Hoggie " but his heart is definitely in the right place! He probably has that mental block where I'll always be "Hoggie" even though he knows now it's Boggie!

He is friends with a guy called Tony Mcgeever, an actor from London who is originally from Edinburgh, a fellow Hibs fan too may I add. Max had mentioned my story and book to Tony and that's where the whole Edinburgh fringe story begins.

Tony contacted me and mentioned he had spoken to Max and wondered if I fancied meeting up in Edinburgh. My initial thoughts were what is he wanting and how much will it cost me?? Most people who have contacted me are after something. My life's savings are non-existent now so I'll hear him out but I'm paying no more money out to people promising me the world!

We met in Edinburgh at the Jolly restaurant of all places. The Jolly was my first proper job at the age of fifteen. Dishwasher duties every Friday and Saturday night. I worked my way up to try my hand at being a waiter too and had a shot at being chef, £10 for Friday and £15 for Saturday. Back in the day £25 a week was a lot of money. It allowed me to buy my own clothes and chip in on a bit of cannabis with my friends. Looking back though it actually kept me off the streets. My friends were becoming increasingly experimental with drugs and I didnt want to indulge.

At least now I had a reason to not buy a bottle of buckfast and a bit of cannabis. The downside was, I quickly became an outcast from the group, missing raves, house parties and mischief.

So Vito the owner of the Jolly met me and Tony at the entrance, his face always lit up when he saw me, "I had a poster of you up in the restaurant", he told me but "someone pinched it". We ordered drinks and food and Tony asked me if I knew why he had asked to meet me. I replied you are a professional actor so maybe something to do with a feature film? He asked me if I had heard of Trainspotting? I replied of course who hasn't? He continued to inform me that Trainspotting was a book and before it became a blockbuster film it was a play.

I had no knowledge of this so was intrigued to hear more. I have been in many West End shows in London including War Horse so how would you feel about me writing a play for the Edinburgh Fringe he asked? I was self-talking straight away thinking how much is this guy wanting for that?? After an hour or so it became clear that he genuinely seemed supportive of my cause to get my story out there. We left the Jolly and Tony headed back to London and me to Fife.

I remember feeling excited at the prospect of a Fringe Show. I said to my wife Steph that the meeting had gone really well, but still no mention of costs. I had a zoom with Tony the following day and asked him straight out. 'How much would this set me back? 'He replied nothing!! I will secure funding, he replied. At this point I realised that I had nothing to lose but potentially everything to gain. We continued video calling and although officially I am a co-scriptwriter of the show, Tony has done all the hard work. Sorting producers, directors, lighting and sound is something I have no clue about.

I really needed someone like Tony to see the importance of my story, and offer the time and expertise to make it a reality.

Finding a venue was a big headache, Covid had meant there was a huge backlog of shows, so for us to secure a venue was going to be difficult. Tony called me and asked if I was sitting down!! Oh here we go I thought! I hate being pessimistic but I am a realist and I'm used to being let down but it still doesn't make it any easier. He proceeded to tell me that he had just come out of a meeting with the Army at the Fringe and they wanted us for their venue!

It was honestly a huge surprise. Turns out, they actually want us to headline for the whole duration of August. I've had a hard time from a small number of soldiers and veterans on social media so this made me feel amazing. Perhaps finally the army would acknowledge my efforts to try and help people, who knows? I certainly won't hold my breath through fear of suffocation. Shortly after, an email comes in from Edinburgh Castle to invite me and Tony as guests of honour for Her Majesty's 96th birthday! A twenty-one gun salute, we had front row seats! It was an honour and privilege to be acknowledged in such a way and it was all thanks to Tony McGeever!

In life, people have taken advantage of my kind nature, they took me for thousands of pounds from my savings. I have trust issues for good reasons, and I'm definitely gullible but I'm learning that people are not always what they seem. To find Tony at a time when I was struggling, and to get support really did restore my faith in humanity.

I can see the Edinburgh fringe being the start of something extraordinarily special. I always had faith in myself. Self belief is real and important for me, so I never quit trying to help. Perhaps my third book, if there is to be one, will be about us globe-trotting around the theatres of this world. I really do hope so!

Sitting in New York having a cuppa with Michael Stipe from REM is a dream, a dream that most people will laugh at. That's ok though, people laughed when I said I'd get clean, people laughed when I said I was joining the Scots Guards and look what happened there! Michael actually has two copies of my book, "Heroin To Hero", both sent with personal letters inside, one was sent to REM headquarters and the other was sent to his sister.

His sister sent me a screenshot of a reply about the story that was done for the Scottish Sun. "'Aww sweet story" he replied with a couple of kisses, thinking the kisses were for his sister and not me but I'll take it.

There is no point trying to put into words what it would really mean to one-day meet him, shake his hand and say thanks for saving my life.

Tony McGeever, incredible talented actor and me

Mum, Dad and Me at the opening show

I'm grateful to the many supporters who bought tickets to see the show

Steph & Cherise in Edinburgh at the start of the show

MEMORIES OF BASIC TRAINING

January 2010, I left Waverley train station in Edinburgh to head down to Catterick to begin my basic training, waving goodbye to my Mum and Dad.

Truth be told, I think they were expecting me home a few days later. Little did they know that I was more determined than ever to achieve the impossible. I had flipped my addiction from heroin to fitness and all the running, cycling, boxing, swimming and weight lifting had really put me in with a good chance of success. Soldiers need to be fit….or so I thought. However, I was to become 3011 2753 Trainee Guardsman Boggie and that was a different kettle of fish.

We were picked up from Darlington train station and loaded onto a coach like something out of bad lads army, Scottish, English, Welsh and Irish accents galore. I couldn't understand what most of them were saying, especially the Welsh. We arrived in Catterick and the sergeant put us all in three ranks for the first time. As they walked along the line to speak to the new recruits it was clear there was going to be a fair amount of banter and piss taking, hair, teeth, clothes and accent, it was all up for discussion. When they got to me the sergeants just laughed, 'how old are you for fuck sake?' I replied, "thirty sergeant"!! They instantly knew who I was to my complete shock. "Are you the smackhead from the east coast?" they asked. Everyone laughed until the sergeant bellowed to keep the noise down. I nodded which was met with a stern look, eventually I said, "yes", and the sergeant replied,"yes sergeant you dick". This was going to be a long seven months I remember thinking.

On the second day we had our mile and a half fitness test, basically a best effort run to gauge our fitness, surrounded by eighteen year old whipper snappers. I remember thinking this is why I trained so hard, please don't embarrass yourself. We took off and quickly, I realised that these guys were starting to breathe a little too heavy. I got my head down and focused on the front runner, he was too quick to catch up but I finished third out of fifty so I was really proud of myself. We met the officers and the sergeant major shortly after finishing.

In the military you get given a time as you pass the finish line and told to line up in the order you came in. It seemed the same questions were going to be asked. How old are you? Are you the young man who had problems? As the officers politely put it. "yes sir", I replied and again there was sniggering. The sergeant major piped up and told everyone they should all be quiet as I had just embarrassed them all!

"Well done Trainee guardsman Boggie, I look forward to hearing about your life on the heroin", officers nodded and they moved on down the line.

I won an award in week two. I actually can't remember the reason but I was given a plaque. It was a memorial plaque from a Welsh guard who had sadly lost his life. It was a shock to hear my name read out but I was quickly becoming a known character amongst the boys and they all respected me after hearing of my struggles in earlier life. Fitness was going to be my strong point as I was soon to realise. We were put into our green kit which consisted of a white buff belt, forage cap and drill boots. Now we will teach you to march, we were told. Ok no worries, how hard can it be? Very difficult as it turned out for me. Initially I was trying to copy my friends next to me but I was a millisecond behind of course and easily noticeable. My body just didn't move the way I wanted and I found drill the most difficult part of basic training. I was showing my determination to learn which didn't go unnoticed. Tik Toking isn't a social media app, it's when your feet and arms go in the same direction at the same time. It looks so funny and unnatural but very common amongst the fresh recruits.

The best way I had it explained was to exaggerate myself walking normally. It took me a long time but I finally got the hang of it. Bayonet drills soon followed, I remember taking a gash out my ear!

Don't ask me how but I remember standing on the drill square feeling liquid dribbling down my ear onto my shirt. I made the mistake of moving and the sergeant gave me a bollocking, and then again for answering back. I learnt from that day that I should never move on parade unless instructed, and certainly keep my big mouth shut. The problem was I was becoming a gobshite in camp, all the staff were great fun at points and allowed me to answer back regularly. I was known as having great morale for the troops. However there is work time and play time and knowing from which is very important. The Welsh Guards sergeant actually liked me and came in later to check my ear was okay.

We were given an SA80 rifle!! Yes that's right I was handed a rifle.

It was my first time handling a firearm. My concern quickly changed from fearing my own drills to fearing some of the bampots around me. "Check this Boggie I'm Rambo!", I was genuinely scared we were getting handed live rounds. First we were taught how to strip the rifle and put it back together, then how to clean it. My problem was, I struggled with all the different names of parts and the cleaning kit. I tried to remember the names but kept getting it wrong, so I started making up my own names. Biggest bloody mistake I made! Big toothbrush, small toothbrush, toothpick, lego block to name a few. The confusion was real. Everyone laughed at my name calling, it was to become my downfall as time went on.

Firing a rifle was a new experience. At the range for the first time I remember lying in the prone position, which is lying on the floor, chest side down, really nervous to fire my first rounds. I kept getting kicked in the head by the Coldstream sergeant, I had a helmet on obviously but it was annoying. 'Keep your finger away from that trigger bawbag' he bellowed, I never listened so he proceeded to kick me until I took notice of my fault. I was never going to be a sharpshooter but I wasn't the worst. In the middle I'd say, I would settle for that. Amazing at physical training, shit at ceremonial drills and just OK at rifle drills. The staff were only interested in my effort so even if I got things wrong they would teach me.

After getting to grips with my rifle drills I was handed a light machine gun!! This was great fun to be honest and I was probably a better shot with it than the rifle. Yet again another weapon system with all new parts to learn, and a new cleaning kit. A huge toothbrush this time!

I remember on one exercise I was the gunner. It was pitch black and we were attacking a position. I needed to change the belt and I genuinely thought I had lost my finger. I put it somewhere it had no business being. Fortunately it wasn't even bleeding, just badly bruised, a bit like my ego. I still had a lot to learn.

If you have read my first book you will know my story is full of dramatic events, over dramatised by my mind, drowning, getting stuck on a mountain, getting bitten by a horse..

One story I never shared was the time I was paralysed. Tactical exercise two. Basically it was a combination of all the things we were taught to become a fighting soldier. I had asked to be a light machine gunner, however I had picked up a bug on the second day. We were on patrol late at night in the middle of nowhere, a heavily wooded area with no way to know my direction other than following the man in front.

Due to my fitness I was always up front usually, on this particular night I had started to fall back. I was sweating more than usual and my breathing became very heavy. I fell back all the way to the last man. I remember seeing the silhouette of my friend's legs in front of me and realised I must keep him in sight or I'll get lost. Over the next 10 minutes I slowly fell way back. I could hear them moving away in the distance and I had to stop to catch my breath. We were issued a radio and I still wasn't clued up with how to communicate with it properly. I knew everyone could hear me if I spoke on it. I decided to stay silent and try my best to catch them up.

Yes you guessed it, I got lost, I now couldn't hear anything and realised that i'm going to have to use this flaming radio. Okay, but first I must rest as I was feeling faint. I took my kit off and let some air into my chest area. As I was lying on my side catching my breath, I felt a very strange feeling. It started with tingling, then a numbness all down my right side and it was spreading. I won't lie, I absolutely shit myself and all thoughts of using the radio properly left my mind. This is an emergency and I need help immediately or I may die.

I picked up my radio and whispered 'mate can you hear me? It's Boggie!! Why I whispered I'll never know, it's not like my mate would hear my whisper but all the officers wouldn't. "Where are you Boggie"? someone asked. "I'm lost and paralysed", I replied. "Stay where you are and we will come find you ya dickhead" someone answered. Ten minutes later I could hear people getting closer. It was pitch black and we were not allowed lights of course as it was a tactical exercise. A torch went on and it shone straight in my face. "Who is that?" the sergeant asked. "It's Boogie sergeant", I replied.

It was another section of Welsh Guards coming in from patrol. The same sergeant who had given me a hard time when I cut my ear. I'm a paralysed sergeant. He shone his torch to my side and said to me, "look you arshole you're lying in a bed of jaggy nettles". I wasn't paralysed after all, which was a relief but I had messed up big time. My sergeant had given me a bollocking for my mistakes, when I replied that I clearly wasn't well he took me round the corner over a small hill and jumped on top of me. It's not the first time I've taken a hiding. I did deserve it for gobbing off though, although this time I had body armour and a helmet on so didn't feel anything.

My sergeant didn't like me, I was too much of a gobshite for him. I later found out he had tried to get me back squadded, which is put back to an earlier week in training, fortunately he was in the minority and it never happened, but my cards were marked with him.

Back in camp after the exercise we had an inspection coming up so it was time to get the iron out. I was a tight arse so I bought an iron from the local Tesco for £11.99. Some of the guys' mothers had bought them the Ferrari of irons so we often shared those. I remember having all my kit squared away, creases in the right places, soles of my boots and trainers scrubbed clean. Just getting ready to get my head down for the night and I went for a piss. I do talk a lot and met a friend so we were chatting away for five or ten minutes in the toilet. When I came out I saw my sergeant in the corridor. "You leave your locker open Boggie"?, he asked. I knew what was coming and I could hear the laughter coming from my room. I walked in to find all my shirts, t-shirts, trousers, laces from my boots and trainers all tied together in knots and hung round the whole room!! It was met with much hilarity and soon all the Welsh, English and Irish trainee guardsmen came along for a look. I was absolutely fuming and our relationship became very stagnant. I respect the chain of command, always have, but he wasn't my favourite person. Of course there is a lesson there. Kit security is important so never leave your lockers open, even if you're only going for a piss. I was up until the early hours with the Ferrari iron so it could have been worse.

I was told that tactical exercise three was going to be my time to shine. After back squadding being mentioned I was certainly on everyone's radar. Basically "Tac Ex 3" is a week of digging trenches. It induces sleep deprivation to see how we all cope. I soon realised how lazy some of the guys were. I swear one of them fell asleep standing up, leaning on the pickaxe!! I had a point to prove, so I got stuck in regardless and it was clear we were falling behind a section. The English,Welsh and Irish had all turned into little rabbits and moles. After two days without any sleep, (except for the pickaxe guy who shall remain nameless) the sergeant came over to speak with me. "How's morale now Boggie"? he asked, "All good sergeant", I replied. I thought he was being wide with me but to my surprise he picked up a pickaxe and said let's do this. The two of us jumped into that trench and double handedly smashed the remaining dirt out. It had been raining for days so we were in a proper state. I remember the sergeant major nodding at me when I looked up so I was glad someone had seen my effort. It was clear I was putting the graft in so on day four I was gifted a half hour rest from digging. Instead I was to go pick up brass, empty shells from the rounds that had been fired. I genuinely feel my fitness saved me from backsquading.

The time had come to start preparing for the passing out parade, I had made it all the way to the end. Seven months of hell, physical and mental hell. We had one parade to do beforehand. I remember standing at the side of the drill square with my red tunic on. Other Scottish regiments were there that day, we all lined up in three ranks facing each other. We were taught we were special in comparison and there were a few daggers thrown about. All the officers and sergeants had made their way onto the drill square and left us alone. Things fell silent until I had a bright idea to lighten the mood. Sons of Scotland I am William Wallce, words of William Wallace from the film Braveheart. Safe to say it certainly lightened up the mood, for us Scottish anyway haha.

The day had finally come when my parents would travel down to Catterick to see my passing out parade. Rehearsals had gone really well and I was confident I knew what I was doing. We had been up all night putting the finishing touches to our white buff belts and bulling our boots. Drama never seems to escape me and the passing out parade would prove to be no different. We were getting ready to set off and I was putting my tweed trousers on and I noticed some of the stitching had started to fray. We wore braces which had put pressure on the tweeds. The stitching hasn't come away completely but I was worried so shouted the sergeant over, he told me to put my green belt on to help hold them up. This is five minutes before marching off for the final time to the drill square. I put my green belt on and joined everyone in three ranks outside",

By the left, quick march, the platoon sergeant bellowed. Off we went en route to the drill square, we could hear the families and it was very exciting. We made it onto the drill square in one piece, As we came to our first halt to face our families I felt the most traumatic snap. My tweeds had given way from my braces!! You literally couldn't write it, or perhaps I can. Yes I was now left without any support for my tweeds other than the green belt I had put on at the last minute. This green belt was the only thing stopping my tweeds falling down to bare my boxer shorts to the crowd.

I managed to get through the rest of the parade but I honestly can't remember too much of it. Luckily, I was always put in the middle or back because my drill wasnt as good as some of the guys. Pictures do exist of my tweeds but I dare not show anyone as I will get ridiculed.

Truth is much of my first book and this book will be scrutinised by the Scots Guards. I've learnt since publishing my first book that it's not about them but more about sharing my story with you lot. My parents were very quiet that day, I only found out from my mum later that they just couldn't get their heads round what they had just witnessed.

From heroin and all that goes with it to this proud standing official Guardsman. It never really sunk in for me either. I very much took the seven months basic training one day at a time, never really thinking about the outcome. I never thought about what would happen when basic training finishes, and what would become of me. I was sent to London for nine months, I really enjoyed my time as a guardsman. You could feel the respect as we went about our duties, even in civilian clothes people seemed to know we were soldiers. Windsor Castle first, then onto Buckingham Palace, St James palace soon followed and finally the Tower of London.

I actually did the Keys Ceremony at the Tower of London, "Halt who goes there?" It's on Youtube if you'd like to look it up, if you don't know what it is. It was a real honour and a privilege to take part in. It's a 700 year old tradition where every night we lock up the tower.

Leaving London was sad, I really found my feet with regards to the drill and started to get too comfortable I suppose. I was always drinking too which was never a problem as far as addiction goes but definitely affected my life.

Returning to Catterick as a Guardsman, not a trainee Guardsman was cool. Everyone was so much more chilled out. The harsh reality bit me on the arse a few months later when my date to deploy to Afghanistan came in. Initially, I was terrified and remember sitting in my room thinking about what I had let myself in for. You have to understand that in my life there have always been dramas, if Afghanistan was to be the same I may not come back. Yes I was fully trained, but until I go I won't know. My friends noticed my mood had dropped so they started visiting me at night to have a joke and laugh about getting shot and who would be carrying who. It was just banter but it really did help bring me round. Unfortunately, or fortunately whichever way you look at it, I broke my back and crushed my spine a couple of months before deployment. I wasn't driving the car!! Yet again more drama in my life but this time it was going to become a proper test of will. A test I would fail at in the following years.

Drug addiction albeit from the doctors this time would rear its ugly head and leave me questioning life. Initially things were okay, I was still a serving soldier, I had the structure still in place. Shave every morning, then go for my swin, acupuncture, rehabilitation courses which taught me how to manage my back issues. I was still part of the team even though I was broken.

It wasn't until I was medically discharged in June 2015 that my problems started to arise. No uniform, no aftercare, left to my own devices. From past experiences I had learnt a lot about drugs, how they could allow me to escape my reality, short term at least. I was able to justify my drug use this time round, not only to my family but more importantly to myself. My family never questioned my drug use although they did notice a downward spiral after my medical discharge.

Physically I was starting to rot.

I became bitter and twisted with the world, jealous of army friends who were being promoted, especially the driver of the car. He made the rank of sergeant very quickly and it was supposed to be me who was first for promotion.

I entered a dark head space which I found unbearable. I couldn't watch any TV programmes which spoke of Afghanistan. All the training and hard work had been for nothing or so I told myself on a daily basis. I couldn't cope so I decided to abuse my meds. Taking tramadol, codeine and diazepam to ease my troubled mind became normal. I knew if I added cannabis to the cocktail it would heighten the effects of all the other drugs so I started buying cannabis which actually made me feel terrible. Engaging with drug dealers again truly was a new low for me. So of course I took more drugs to forget.

Before long I started to notice that my headaches were turning into migraines.

My bouts of dizziness were becoming more frequent and my chest and gut really had become very painful. I never spoke of it to anyone other than my wife and even then I held some information back.

I was scared and didn't want anyone who loves me to be the same. Dizziness was definitely the scariest, I'd never suffered with this before. The room would spin, I'd feel sick and on many occasions I had to stop and lie down where I was because if I didnt i felt I would pass out. Yet again, I indulged with more drugs to escape the fear, the same drugs I believed were causing it.

My saving grace was my wife.
When I had become suicidal all those years ago I remember living alone. Nobody to talk to or offload my worries onto, this time around I had someone who didn't

understand but was willing to listen and support. I wasn't as heavily depressed as before but I knew it could head that way.

Having my wife there everyday allowed me to stay stronger than I would have been. To live in your own head whilst suffering is really a terrible thing, the only person to talk to is yourself and I have nothing nice to say. My self talk had turned to the old ways,

I had a reason to live, my wife and stepdaughter loved me and I felt it everyday.

At times, it made it more difficult because I was so engulfed with my addiction that my happiness was surrounded by thoughts of tramadols. My whole life dictated to by my drug consumption.

Basic training

Me in basic training.

In Canada living the dream!

CROWDFUNDING AND CHARITIES

I actually hate crowd funding and for several reasons. Firstly after finishing my first book I set up a charity boxing event which was held in the Yorkshire Dales. The idea was to host the event and set up a go fund me to recoup my costs. In theory it would work, if everything materialised that I was promised then it would have been a success.

Unfortunately, this was going to be an expensive lesson. I organised all the boxers, travel, equipment and headed to yorkshire. Set up a go fund me and posted videos everyday to explain what we were doing. I made the mistake of spending a little over £3000 of my savings to put the event on, Go fund me raised just £475. To this day I'm out of pocket almost £3000.

An expensive lesson to learn, my wife did warn me but I didn't listen. Basically, I was promised the world and none of it materialised. I was beginning to understand that people generally don't care about what I'm trying to achieve. If everyone who apparently supported me had put £1 in, then I would have raised money for homelessness in the UK instead of ending up in the red.

I understand sometimes I come across as pessimistic, to be honest it is. I have good reason not to trust anyone I don't know. What counts is that I haven't given up. People tell me homeless people are scammers, homeless charities tell me that there aren't any rough sleepers anymore, homeless people are druggies, homeless people all choose to be on the street.

Opinions are like arseholes…everyone has one. Some of the points made are accurate but not all. What about the genuine homeless? Do we just forget about them because of the scammers?

I've never liked asking for people's money, I have had to do it on occasions. People ask about "Just giving" pages or "Go fund me" and I always say that the only way to support me is by buying the book. Truth is I feel really let down.

Most people on social media are fake in my opinion. They blow smoke up your hoop because they want attention. Don't get me wrong there are lots of amazing people I've met too, but ninety per cent are full of shit. I would like to say that's me done with all the negativity but it's not.

Skip to the next chapter if i'm offending you as I understand some people can't handle the truth, I wont say any names though.

Charities make money from the misery of people, why would they want to actually fix the issues when their lavish lifestyles rely upon it? People are delusional if they think their donation actually reaches the people who need help, a very small portion will receive help and the media will promote the hell out of it.

Charities are big business, I understand they have costs, fuel, electricity and wages are all acceptable. What's not acceptable is for lots of these people taking six figure salaries for sending a few emails whilst people are dying on our streets. It's a well researched fact that most people are driven by money. The world we live in is full of greed, full of helping out if it benefits you. I've been very gullible in my life, even in recent years.

I've invested in people only to be bumped out of thousands of pounds, one of which I served with in the Scots guards, £5000 to be exact. Such a shame that people let greed take over their morals and integrity. Then you have people in this world who are just nasty, plain and simple nasty. This book isn't about these people so I'm going to move on. I'm merely acknowledging it.

Let's move onto the next chapter and leave all the nasties where they belong far behind me.

DRUGS AND STIGMA

Everything that I write about drugs is just my opinion. I feel I have knowledge of drugs because of my lived experiences. These are what I'll share with you.

If I mention a specific drug it's because I've had a run in with it.

Ketamin, legal highs for example I've never taken so it would be foolish to write about them. On my prison visits I'm hearing a lot about how spice is taking over as the new drug of choice. I'm intrigued about this drug but I certainly won't be trying it just to find out what all the hype is about. From what I've witnessed it seems to change a person, it seems to be a powerful mind altering drug.

The closest thing I've taken to this sort of change is LSD and magic mushrooms. No amount of testimonies from people or watching videos will ever give me a true understanding.

Heroin is a mind altering drug but doesnt change you like what magic mushrooms does. I found heroin to be a relaxing drug. I wanted to be left alone to enter a world where nothing mattered. The sleep-like state I would enter would have people thinking I was fast asleep but I often found myself earwigging. I even had slavers dribbling from my mouth but wouldn't move, 'look at the state of Boggie what a mess'. I heard many conversations about me whilst I was out of it. Truth is I didn't care, I was just enjoying the peace and quiet in my head.

Early on I realised that if I actually fell asleep it would be a waste of money. Waking up realising I had lost that feeling was horrible. The hunt for money and the drug would commence all over again, Groundhog day. So I always fought against sleeping. Another of my problems was that I had become a greedy drug user. I never physically needed drugs but if I had them I would take them. This left me in some situations when I felt lucky to be alive, especially when tablets came on the scene. To chase the dragon you have to prepare everything and then actually smoke it.

Tablets however are gone in two seconds. I had no reason to swallow twenty codeines whilst I sat chasing the dragon but I had convinced myself it would be a stronger hit. Like I said, it was sheer greed.

Prior to getting my drugs I would make a plan to make them last for a specific time.

These plans never worked and left me cold turkey on many occasions. I remember one Christmas Eve we had been to pick up our bags of heroin, we all got two or three bags of heroin each.

I had three so I was sorted until the day after boxing day. Christmas is a time for family and this would be great, no stressing, being able to wake up not worrying about getting our fix. We all went home early that night, everyone was sorted individually so we didn't need each other. I remember the filmSaving Private Ryan being on the box.

I cracked open the first bag and it was a terrible deal. Stuck it on the foil and began chasing the dragon. The plan was to watch the film then go to sleep, hopefully waking up on Christmas morning with some heroin still on the foil. I had actually fallen asleep after one hour of trying to watch the film.

I remember waking up and checking the foil, it was all gone! Of course, I didn't need anymore but I still had two bags stashed away and my mind quickly convinced me to take a small part of the second bag. Rather than farting about with separating powder I just put the whole second bag on the foil. I ended up watching the rest of the film. I lay with my eyes closed but not asleep. Everytime I came around I reached for the foil. Just a couple more lines I told myself.

We were now into the early hours of Christmas day. I finally fell asleep and woke to the noise of my family banging on my bedroom door which was locked of course, ``Paul it's Christmas'' my dad shout Come see what Santa has brought you. Not a bag of heroin I remember thinking. I looked down at the blackened foil sheets to my horror. I was reminded that I'd actually finished that second bag. No worries, I had one left and if I can split it up I will manage the next two days. I opened my presents then did my usual which was to disappear back to my room, lock the door and my mind quickly turned to the third bag.

I wasn't withdrawing so no need to open it yet. Of course, I would want to just check if it was a better deal than the others. Having a couple of lines and leaving it for later, seemed a great idea at the time. I opened it, smoked it all, fell asleep, and was woken up by my brothers to say Christmas dinner was ready. It would have been around 3pm. Again, on waking up I looked down to check the foil. It was all gone!

The only thing I had left was the oil that had gathered into my tooth, which is the silver foil tube used for smoking the heroin. It would have a few lines at most in it which wouldn't hold me for the whole day and night. Fear and anxiety had taken over. No money, no heroin, no way of getting any.

I skipped Christmas dinner which probably broke my parents hearts. I got dressed and decided to walk the streets to see if I could find anyone who could help me out.
I thought I'd be the only greedy one and be left alone on Christmas night. If you're thinking why wouldn't you just go to your friends houses who you knew had heroin then you don't know my so called friends. They were not like that. Phones went off

and if you went to the door you were met with stern looks from parents. My only chance was me not being the only greedy addict.

I walked around Craigentinny a few times until I met one of my so-called friends. ``Yep smoked them all and we are not the only ones, the rest are already away for more". I was not surprised, not the fact they had smoked all theirs too, but the fact they had left without us. I knocked on the neighbour's door and asked to borrow another £20. This was not the first time asking nor would it be the last. I think they took pity on me because it was Christmas. I made my false promises of repayment soon and left with my £20. Problem now was finding a dealer who was selling on Christmas day. We were told not to try doors or windows on Christmas as the dealers wouldn't sell hence why we had bought three bags all at once.

The person who had all the connections for the dealers was already away with some of the others to try to get some. Basically, the ringleader of our group held all the cards when it came to addresses and phone numbers. This was a ploy to become very important and it worked, "If you go to the door and they don't recognise you they will rob you or possibly stab you" we were told.

So on this particular night it was me and one friend left behind. We started the few miles trek to the area of the dealers. We knew the rough locations so the plan was to wait outside and ask someone as they left the stairwell. We approached Bingham tunnel which was notorious for trouble makers hanging about. The long way round would take too long. Withdrawals had set in so we decided to run the gauntlet. It was dark which always added to the danger. It was actually quite busy, but mostly people were on their new bicycles from Santa. I remember seeing four figures walking towards us and they looked dodgy. I always wore a jumper with two jackets, the exterior always had a hood. I lifted my hood up and pulled my new scarf from Santa up over my mouth. '"We run and don't fight,' I told my friend.

As they came closer we met under the bridge of all places. I never held eye contact whenever I went into the area. I knew I would give up if I had money and needed a heroin look, which is likely to get me robbed or worse. I put my head down until I heard a voice, 'Alright' I instantly recognised the voice, it was our ring leader. I pulled my hood down and laughed. The instant relief was clear and it was short lived, "Did you get anything I asked?'
"Yeah but they only had a couple left", he replied. I asked if he would come with us to try to get them. He refused, which started a huge argument. I called him all the names under the sun, he had shat on us big time. They had their bags and that's all that mattered, even the offer of some of our bags couldn't convince him.

Hood's backup and off we went into a fit of rage. I wouldn't forget it, that's for sure. It was only a short walk to the dealer's area. We went to the stairwell and stood at the corner. We needed a number between 1 and 6. Ring leader wouldn't tell us so we waited. A young lad came out the stairwell so we approached him with our hoods down. We asked if he got it and he replied yes, Which number mate I asked. 5 he replied. So far things were going ok, We had a house number and we had money. Only one person goes to the door so another argument broke out about who should go to the door.

Eventually because I had a score (£20) and my friend only had a tenner he was going to the door. I handed him the £20 note and he handed me his tenner. I walked around the block to try not look so suspicious, with my hood and scarf up, who was I trying to kid? If I get stabbed then hopefully the jumper and 2 jackets would save me. Wearing so many layers also made me look like I had a bigger frame than I actually did. I was a skinny young man trying to look big. I walked only once round the block and I saw my friend. He couldn't hide his excitement. A complete spring in his step.

First time ever going to a heroin dealer and he looked so happy.

His excitement quickly spread to me as he showed me the bag of heroin. It was huge, double what we normally get!! Must be because it's Christmas we joked. We quickly marched all the way home, stopped at the garage to get tobacco, two kit kat biscuits for the foil and a bottle of fizzy juice. That left me skint now but who cares! The bag was huge and worth celebrating with some tobacco for a chaser. A chaser is something we do regularly.

You inhale the heroin smoke and then take a drag of a cigarette, if we were to flush a joint of cannabis but that was rare as all our money went on heroin. It was Christmas night so we couldn't go to each other's house so we headed to the high rise flats at Lochend, a usual haunt. If a ringleader is there I will punch him, I told my friend. Fortunately, there was nobody there.

We started to set up everything, my friend set up the tooter using one of the kit kats, I took the other and began to flatten it out taking extreme care not to rip it. I proceeded to burn the chemicals from the back of the foil. Crazy when you think we took so much care to remove the chemicals from the foil to put heroin in our systems but it was the done thing. I took the pristine flat sheet of kit kat foil and held it out, my friend carefully opened the bag and tipped it into a crease I had created to collect the powder. I took my lighter and tested the flame size which was also something very important to do. If it was too big, it could scorch the heroin. We had learnt this the hard way on previous occasions.

Everything was ready to go, so I took the tooter from my friend and placed it in my mouth.

I began to heat the brown powder until it turned into a brown blob of liquid making sure to inhale as much smoke as I could handle. It was the biggest blob of heroin I had ever seen. This would last us for a couple of days, no of course it wouldn't, it was gone in the next two hours. Boxing day's fix was going to be different, I was still fuming at the ring leader so we decided that night we would go ourselves to the dealer. No dramas that night, straight up and down, same stairwell, same number 5 door, same deal. The following days we forgave the ring leader and began to hang around together again. Everyone chipped in so it made sense to stick together. Another huge argument was brewing though.

We all chipped in to get a couple of bags to share amongst six of us. Same area, same stairwell, same number 5 door, not the same deal nor was the ringleader away for five minutes. He returned after twenty minutes so a very anxious bunch of friends, eyes pupils were pinned and glazed and we could all tell he had a smoke. Let me see the deal I asked instantly, "not here", he replied with anger. We headed back to the high rise flats, this time though we sneaked into my friend's bedroom. We all sat on his bed and all eyes were on the ringleader, he went into his sock and pulled the bag out. "That looks a good deal", a few of the guys mentioned.

I took it and turned to my friend who had been to the same dealer a few times over Christmas. 'Youre a fucking dickhead', I bellowed. Everyone started on me as we were not supposed to be in my friend's house. He is bumping us. I told everyone, I had my friend confirm that the size was about half what we had previously received. Also the way the bag was, it had a single mark to keep it closed which if we had not received the previous bags, we would have thought that was normal. From that day forward we were at each other's throats. He knew I was onto him and he hated me for it.

The time would come when I would have to go to the dealers myself. This was not a choice, more of a necessity. I was working and by the time I finished I was starting to feel cold turkey setting in. I wore a shirt and tie for my work so I could be mistaken for a police officer potentially, or someone official looking, which could end up getting me stabbed. I didn't have far to walk from getting off the bus. I had my £20 at the ready. All I had to do was get to the number 5 door, then back to the bus stop as I had a day saver ticket for my work.

I built the anticipation up so much I thought I was going to vomit or perhaps that was the need for heroin. My shirt was soaked and sticking to my back, I took my tie off in a plea to make myself less official looking. I tapped the letterbox and a little hand popped out, I placed the £20 in the palm and said 'one please'. The hand disappeared and for a short time I thought I was being bumped.
What was I going to do, certainly not start a commotion in the stairwell. It didn't matter as the same little hand appeared shortly after and I put the palm of my hand

out and a bag of heroin was placed. What was all the drama about? This was easy, they even said thanks through the letterbox.

No questions, no knives, no drama.

All that had been told to us from the ring leader had been a way of retaining our need for him. Now I can get my own drugs and I started to distance myself from the group more and more. It's sad to say but some of my happiest memories are of heading home with a bag of heroin in my sock.

Of course I would still need my friends because £20 wasn't always easy to come by so we often went halves. We no longer needed the ring leader though and before long everyone was going to number 5 door for their fix.

A few weeks later I would have to put my tail between my legs and go see the ring leader once again. Number five had been busted by the police and the windows were boarded up. I asked for the address of the other dealers and I was told no so I knew what was coming. I had no choice but to hand over my £20 and receive what was given.

This time there were no single marks but the deal was terrible and the bag looked like it had been hampered with, you can tell by how much powder was around the edges when you opened it up. Of course, I voiced my displeasure but I had to be careful, he could just refuse to get me it and then I'd be completely stuck.

Eventually I started to recognise the same faces and befriended some of them. I remember sitting in a dealers house, about 20 people were all crammed into the living room, one guy was manning the front door as the dealer sat chasing the dragon, he had just picked up and we had to wait until he had tested it, with heroin the inevitable was going to happen, he smoked too much and started to dribble from his mouth, I remember sitting on the carpet on my own with a bunch of heroin users who also looked ill.

The dealer came round and looked at me, I had already handed my £20 over so I was reliant on the guy from the door remembering, 'you from Craigentinny he asked?' Yes mate, I replied and he just nodded. I wasn't first in the queue and it took him forever to make my bag up, stopping every five minutes to chase a few lines.

I got my bag and quickly marched all the way home. These occurrences were to become more frequent. I was getting known in the area which turned out to be a good thing. I was heading home one night on my own and a group of lads stopped me. I saw a knife and shat myself, not literally but I was touching cloth. Give me your money, one lad asked. I thought about running but they had surrounded me. Was I about to find out if my jumper and two jackets would save me?

I didn't have any money, all I had was a bag of heroin in my sock that I'd just bought. I began to empty my pockets and to my surprise I heard a voice from one of the lads, 'leave him he is okay.' It was the guy I had sat next to on the carpet a few nights previously. I never said a word, just walked away. I did see him again and thanked him for helping me out that night.

From that day onwards every time we saw each other we waved and all his friends began to wave too which made me feel a lot safer when I was in the area. It was one of those friends who would set me up. Intentionally or not he led me into a house where I was sold brick dust. I knew they carried knives so I smoked the brick dust in the hope they had put some heroin in it, of course they didn't. It was actual brick dust, but the orange tint gave it away. Doesn't matter how friendly people seem, nobody was to be trusted.

My life had become very hectic and a need for money to fund my addiction was starting to take over. I had borrowed from everyone who I could. I was working but that would come to an end too. Smoking heroin in the work toilets everyday was never going to last.

I was sacked and went back to the street.

Everyone I knew was stealing from supermarkets to fund their addictions, a few of them had taken to robbing people and I really didn't want to become that person. I was given a lifeline by a guy I went to school with. He tapped my door one day to deliver a £25 bag of cannabis. He then pulled out a nine bar, the biggest block of cannabis I'd ever seen. Nine ounces to be exact, it had a little fish stamp on it. He said he would give me this to sell. All I had to do was give him an amount of cash in one weeks time.

I quickly did the maths and worked out I could earn £250 so I decided to take it. He dealt with some seriously dodgy people so I knew it was a risk. I'm not justifying it but it was the lesser of all evils in my eyes, I could find my heroin addiction and have some cannabis to smoke too.

I knew everyone in the area who smoked cannabis so basically, I gave out better deals so everyone would come to me, I began doing "chucky" too which is letting people pay me at a later date. It actually worked out very well in the beginning and I became known for selling the best deals. Unfortunately I was offered valium to sell and that's when things went downhill. I swallowed blues (10mg) tablets like they were smarties and forgot who I had chuckied out too.

People began to take advantage of my state of mind and some nasties started to show up at the door.

I was probably robbed and didn't even realise. Threats were made and I remember starting to put a hammer behind the front door and under my pillow at night. Fear caused me to only venture out when it was necessary.

18 years old after taking heroin.

FEELING LIKE A KING

I remember having the biggest bundles of cash. I was selling cannabis and valium which earned me a lot of money. This made me feel like a king at times.

A king of my tiny little castle in Lochend but a king nonetheless.

I had wealth and everyone wanted to know me because I gave the best deals. Reality was, I was nothing but a two-bit drug dealer trying to justify an existence. I was able to fund my heroin addiction quite easily, I was beginning to take quite a cocktail of drugs. I'd always enjoyed downers more than uppers for some reason. A friend had asked me to look after pure amphetamine for him as he was at risk of being busted by the police.

I was already in trouble if I got busted, so I didn't see an issue with hiring out a shelf in my freezer to store it. I didn't ask how much there was, I just agreed to help him out. I remember he arrived with a brown leather bag, put it up in the bunker and opened it. I gasped at the size of the iceberg. It was the size of a bowling ball!!!

I was going to have a hard time passing this off as personal use if the police did bust me. He told me I can take 1-gram a day to help him. I'd taken it before but finances had never allowed me to buy it often. I now had access to my own cannabis and valium, I was able to buy my own heroin from my own dealer now so I was all set. I began taking amphetamine and really enjoyed the feeling. It gave me confidence I'd never experienced with any other drug. Even Ecstasy was a little too strong for me at times, Amphetamine I knew where I was at all the time. My body must have been totally confused with all the uppers and downers. I really did feel on top of the world whilst taking amphetamine, I seemed happier than usual and talked a lot. Confidence increase meant I started to venture out more. I didn't believe anyone would notice I was speeding out my nut, of course I was wrong.

It was clear I was on something other than heroin or valium. An opportunity to sell some would soon crop up, although it wasn't mine to sell, I was weighing in to finding new customers for my friend. Couple of months later, he picked up his stash and I got my freezer back. It was a relief because I was always careful about storing too many drugs in the house all at once. Threats from dealers and people grassing me up to the police were always on my mind. I had a mindset that I had nothing to lose, perhaps being locked up would get me off the heroin. I often found myself daydreaming and fantasising about a life away from heroin, I believed it was never going to be achievable so I accepted my fate.

I had decided a car would be a great idea, I'd lost my drivers licence years before due to an accident in Portobello. I had left the scene of an accident because we all had drugs and a few days later, I was pulled over by the police. I admitted it was me who was driving and the rest is history as they say. I had lost my freedom of the open road but I was more concerned about drugs so probably a good thing. I could drive but would never get my licence back.

I decided to buy a car to make my life easier. Abide by the law whilst driving and hopefully not get pulled over. I know what you'll be thinking at this point and you're exactly right! I was an arsehole who didnt care about myself or anyone else. Too self indulgent to give anyone else a second thought. A horrible existence and a horrible memory to write about it to be honest.

It's true, so I feel like I need to share how pathetic I was. Lording it up because I was a cannabis dealer and cutting about like "Billy Big Baws". Truth is, I was a sad individual waiting to die. I knew my time on this earth would be short so I'm going to keep getting wasted until I eventually don't wake up. I did have remorse and feelings of guilt and shame for the things I did, the person I became. My best friend always rectified those thoughts though. Heroin was my best friend. Sad but so true.

I did buy a car and I actually got a job as a delivery driver for a takeaway. I didn't need the money but I enjoyed it. It allowed me to have a reason to only take enough drugs to stop me withdrawing. I of course had no business driving on the road. I'm far from proud of the things I've done but I did learn from my mistakes in time. Thankfully, I never killed anyone because I don't think I would have been able to live with myself.

Drug use would cause me to lose my job because like I stated earlier in the book, I was a greedy addict. Convincing myself I was okay to drive when it was clear to everyone who saw me that I was wasted. It would turn out that I'd get many little jobs in a delusional attempt to better myself but they all ended the same way.

LITERALLY SHITTING MYSELF

Everyone has different traumatic events in life, I spoke about pissing myself in secondary school being a traumatic event for me. What I never mentioned was my tales of actually shitting myself. Not the skid mark kind either. These were full blown jobbies that crusted themselves on my pants or boxer shorts. It wouldn't have been so traumatic if nobody had seen me but of course many people did.

I was a 7 year old young lad who had joined the Beevers then followed later by the Cubs and then Scouts. I remember going away to camp with my dad and all the other kids and parents for the weekend. It was at Bonaly near Edinburgh if I remember right. It was an amazing experience because I had my dad all to myself which had never happened before, Things started well, we played games like throwing the egg to each other, All kids and parents lined up on opposite sides. You throw the egg to your parents and they take a few steps back and return the egg.
Last person to not crack the egg wins. My dad was always super competitive in everything he did so I better not let him down. We had never really played sports where you needed to catch anything. Golf, Snooker and Football were our sports of choice. I was not a very good goalkeeper anyway, too scared of the ball hurting me to be honest. Same to be said when learning to header the football. I was known by my dad and brothers.

Anyway an egg was smaller and surely wouldn't hurt me so we passed the first few rounds no problem, So did everyone else to be fair. As we got further apart we started to lob the egg to give ourselves a better chance of catching it. I saw the egg coming, it was sunny but it wasn't in my eyes; I put my hands up to collect the egg as before, but this time it smashed all over me! I did a little dramatic dance to shake all the slimy egg white off my arms whilst laughing, I could hear lots of laughter but my dad wasn't impressed, 'that was an easy catch' he would tell me.

Disapproval all over his face, It was nothing new though he had been trying to teach us to play sports from my earliest memories. We went to the shower block to get me cleaned up and again, I remember feeling all the attention on me and I loved it. I never purposely cracked the egg though just for attention.

I was told to go and start sawing logs for firewood after dinner. It was still very sunny. A fellow beaver helped me as it was a two way saw. I remember feeling like I needed a number 2. I knew where the toilets were so I didn't have that as an excuse. For some reason I still don't know to this day I thought I could keep holding it in. I was wrong!! I was wearing football shorts that were far too big for me, probably my dads' but they had a tie cord so they wouldn't fall down. We were sawing and I remember the feeling of clenching my bum cheeks together in a vain attempt to stop the inevitable. Because of the shorts my friend who was sawing with me started to scream! "Ewww Paul's shitting himself" he bellowed so everyone close by could hear. I was totally traumatised, quickly jumped up and headed for the shower block. I was soon followed by my dad who was mortified and pissed off. He came armed with a carrier bag to put his soiled football shorts in, I don't think I was bothered about the shorts more the embarrassment I had caused.

I think the leaders of the group must have had a word with everyone because the nickname 'shitey pants' never materialised. Kids are cruel so that's the reason I believe it was spoken about and everyone told not to bring it up. If I had been scared by watching my friend shit himself I would have probably taken the piss.

This wasn't an isolated incident; it became clear over the following years that I would continue to hold my number 2s in and fail. Playing football at Seafield football pitches it happened again. I had bright yellow shorts on, I was in the middle of a game and remember the same feeling that I needed to poo. Again I thought I'd be able to hold off but the shit began showing its ugly head. I thought I'd managed to cut it off without making too much of a mess and continued to play football. I remember at half time I went to the golf course toilets to clean myself up. I could feel the wetness so I knew lots had come out. I scraped as much off my pants as I could but those toilets were notorious for having no toilet paper, so I soon went through a roll or 2 trying to clean myself using water from the sink. When there was no paper left I went to the mirror to check myself.

There was a huge brown mark on my yellow shorts and my heart sank. I had no way of getting home without being noticed. I didn't stay too far away but I certainly wasn't going back for the second half. Perhaps everyone just thought it was a dirt mark from sliding tackles but the smell was pretty bad. I headed across the golf course to try and avoid people, I got into my house and headed straight for the shower, My mum shouted asking who it was? I replied it's just me. She wanted to know why I was home early. My parents always encouraged us to be out the house as youngsters, probably because me and my brothers fought constantly. I never answered her so it only made her more suspicious I think. My pants and yellow shorts lying on the ground my mum entered the bathroom which I had not locked. She mumbled something when she saw my shorts and left with them and returned with clean pants and jogging bottoms. I was often asked what happened but I'd always shrug my shoulders and reply ' I don't know' .

When people speak of childhood trauma being a reason for their drug addictions I am shocked to hear of what some people have gone through. I have definitely had it easy in my young life. My parents did everything possible to give us the best they could. They loved and cared for us and lots of people were not so lucky. I fully understand why lots of addicts would choose heroin as a way of escape, a way of forgetting. I was traumatised as a kid, most self inflicted by my own mind. Pissing and shitting myself didn't help of course and bits of bullying but I was lucky that's all I had to deal with.

All mind altering drugs offer the user a way of escape in the short term, It's clear there is not enough understanding regarding addiction in this world. As a human looking for escape for whatever reason and receiving the desired effect from their drug of choice it's very difficult to not want to have that same amazing feeling again. Problem is of course, with a continued use of certain drugs they become less effective as the first time, you're left chasing that first ever feeling and failing every time. If you take double the amount, yes, it will give you a greater buzz but you'll never reach that first feeling again, for lots of people that won't stop them trying and I can testify I was one of them.

Let's not forget the main reason it's so dangerous to try drugs for the first time. If you're unfortunate enough to find one that blows your mind and you fall in love with that feeling, then addiction will soon follow, and addiction is a whole different kettle of fish.

Lots of uneducated people believe it's simply a physical addiction and if you go through detox you will be home and dry. I can assure you this couldn't be further from the truth. Addiction is a mental problem, not a physical one, Yes of course there are physical problems to go through. Cold Turkey is hell on earth for anyone unfortunate to find themselves there. The reason relapse figures are so high across the globe is because, if you only work on the addiction side of things then you're only combatting the physical side of addiction.

Learning who we are, acknowledging what mistakes and bad choices we have made are crucial. The most crucial of all of them is an understanding why we took drugs in the first place. Only when we do this can we fight back in our minds when moments of weakness appear, which they do for everyone. The reason I have never come close to relapsing on heroin is because I know who I am. I understand it's actually my choice, I understand I could easily let my mind trick me at any time to take heroin. I took the option away of taking heroin again 18 years ago and I'm living proof that what I did works.

The mindset of most addicts is that they don't genuinely believe they can get clean, they may voice it until they are blue in the face like what I did but deep inside they have given up. They are hoping they can get clean as opposed to knowing they can and that's a huge difference. I won't give up trying to help, everyday I'm dealing with addicts on social media who are so negative about their lives, past, present and future.

The idea that they can actually turn it around is absolute nonsense to them.

They may say they are listening to you but they are merely hearing your voice and not grasping what I'm saying. The mind is the key to everything good you could have in this life, and it's your choice.

I have helped lots of people reduce their drug use and even some to get clean but they are in the minority unfortunately at the moment. I will reach more as time goes by because I believe in what I'm teaching. It has to come from within the addict to change. It comes from a willingness to hold your hands up and be truthful. It comes from our minds.

One thing I see a lot of is people claiming to be clean, making statements like 'I've been clean for 5 years. This is an amazing achievement for anyone but I see it slightly different in some situations.

A heroin addict still taking methadone or codeine is not clean. They are clean from heroin for 5 years. There is a big difference in these statements. I'm not taking away anything from anyone breaking away from heroin and using other opiates because that is a huge achievement. What I am saying is that you're replacing one opiate drug for another. You're still an addict and you must acknowledge this fact.

Be proud of yourself but don't be content. You can get clean and break away from drug addiction entirely. We can recover, we do recover, we can even thrive in recovery. I am thriving in recovery, I will always be a recovering heroin addict even when I know I'll never take it again. This is my truth. I own it and I'm proud of what I'm doing now.

All I want is for other people to feel how I feel. It's the greatest feeling in the world to get clean.

Me, first day at primary school.

Me, first day at secondary school

SCHOOL VISITS

I recently went to a high school with Tony to talk about my life. It was a two hour drive south from Fife which wasn't too bad.

It gave me an opportunity to talk about the fringe show. Tony had been up all night writing a script for what he wanted to say. I have never written a script because for me it comes across better if I'm just naturally talking. I don't need to think about what questions will be asked because all my answers are from my lived experience, hence the reason for our invitation. I spoke to the teachers beforehand and they told me to just be myself.

This is all I can be, this is all I want to be so I'm very comfortable. Nerves are normal of course, and as we approached the school Tony had gone quiet. I won't lie, I found it very amusing. As we approached the assembly area we would be addressing everyone. I don't think myself or Tony expected to see so many people. There was an eerie silence as we stood behind the door listening to the teacher introduce us.

The seating area was like something you would see at a concert. I'll need to ask Tony if it's okay to mention this because I don't want to embarrass him. If you're reading this then Tony has agreed haha. I looked down at Tonys. hands as I asked if he was nervous. His hands were shaking so badly, he was gripping his speech so hard, haha. I'm sorry but I found it extremely funny and laughed out loud.

A little bit he replied, I was nervous too of course but clearly not as much. We stepped out in front of the sea of kids and teachers and all eyes were on us. Again I couldn't stop grinning because I knew how nervous Tony had become. He lifted his script up and began speaking, Using all the floor space in true professional actor fashion. First five minutes it was clear he was nervous. He actually mentioned it in his opening statement. Telling everyone who he was, Tony has performed in front of thousands of people in theatres before but nothing quite like this he told everyone.

We had fifteen minutes each to do our speech. After five minutes Tony found his stride and began increasingly relaxed. Telling stories of how he was told he would never be an actor.. He spoke about me like I was something special which made me a little embarrassed. I didn't have a clock to look at but I remember thinking, "hurry up Tony, that's way more than fifteen minutes"!

He had found his groove and was amazing to watch but I wanted to talk as well, as you all know I can.. Eventually he passed it over to me, "Now you'll hear from the man himself, if you think my story is amazing wait until you hear Paul's story".

"Cheers Tony", I replied as I stepped up to the centre of the stage. I knew I wasn't holding back nor did I think I should. I first said hello to everyone. "Drugs are bad, say NO to drugs", and then I walked off stage. Of course, I shortly returned.

"This was my education on drugs when I was your age!" I proceeded to tell everyone I used to be a smackhead, a heroin user from Edinburgh. I have a book but don't make the wrong judgement of me. I did turn it around, I did end up as a Guardsman but I was extremely lucky, I've lost lots of family and friends, some in recent months to drug addiction issues.

I always have to get this point across first in all my school visits. It has the potential to send the wrong message. He was a heroin addict who ended up a soldier so if I end up on heroin I can still become something? Of course they potentially could, but prevention is better than the cure. I'm there to tell the hard brutal truth, the majority of my friends that I hung out with as a youngster are either still on heroin, locked up or dead. I was indeed lucky.

I could look into people's eyes and there were a lot of nervous looks, some giggling as I mentioned the word "smackhead", a few jaws dropped as I proceeded to tell a bit of my story. As my thirteen minutes came to an end (Tony had stolen two of my minutes) I made a few hard hitting statements about the likelihood of kids in front of me becoming addicts. Scotland is getting worse, not better. When I'm in the zone it's difficult to interrupt. The teacher kept looking at me. I knew he was trying to tell me my time was up but I wasn't quite finished haha. I took my extra two minutes and another five for good measure. The teacher walked up as everyone applauded, told everyone that Paul and Tony are here to answer questions so take advantage of them being here. I apologised for running over and was told it's not a problem and it's an amazing story.

We then had a short break before we went into individual classrooms to answer questions and talk more in depth about drug addiction, mental health issues and the power of the mind, to educate what the mind actually is. At first the kids were very shy and nervous. The teachers left me and Tony alone in the classroom but it was clear they were all in little gangs. Nobody really wants to ask a question through fear of being laughed at. I asked them questions which helped break the ice. After one kid would ask a question it opened up the floor for others. Either me or Tony answered the questions and it felt amazing to be helping in such a way.

One question I was asked by a little girl at the back of the classroom was 'Do you think drugs had an impact on you being a deadbeat dad?' All the kids gasped and so did Tony I think. This wasn't my first rodeo answering difficult questions so as much as I wasn't prepared for it I answered it quickly and with confidence. ' Yes drugs most definitely played a huge role in me becoming a deadbeat dad, This is something i will never forget nor forgive myself for but it can't be changed, it's who I am and i own my mistakes. What I can do is try to make up for my mistakes, this is something I have control over, I can't change the past' I replied.

It seemed to be received well. It was a great question that most people wouldn't ever dare ask but some kids have no filter. I'm glad she asked it because it lets the kids realise they can ask me literally anything. I explained that on my last school visit one of the kids had asked me "How do you think your parents felt when they found out you nearly committed suicide?'   Heartbroken and possibly ashamed, it's something that happened and all I can do is try to make them proud was my answer that day, explaining that I can't turn the clock back. All I can do is move forward and learn.

I really enjoy going to schools, you never know nor will I ever know how many kids are impacted with my visit. My brutal way of explaining how dangerous drugs actually are, reasons for taking them and how to prevent becoming an addict. Some kids were already drinking and using drugs so I had a few harsh words to make them think. Addiction can happen to anyone, you are not immune!!

It's not just the kids being educated but also the teachers. Crazy to think that these intelligent people have anything to learn from me but the truth is they do. Everyday is a school day after all, the moment we think we know it all in life is the moment we fail.

I look forward to more school visits and no two visits will ever be the same unlike my message. Drugs are bad, you should say no to drugs! I feel as a youngster that there wasn't enough education for my generation so I choose to try to do something about it. Not one kid in that school knew what chasing the dragon was, or if they did they didnt raise their hand, perhaps due to embarrassment.

Some teachers don't know what it was, teachers should be educated on what drug paraphernalia to look out for, also for some of the tell tale signs of someone using drugs.

Kirkcaldy school visit

Dumfries school visit

HOPE AND INSPIRATION

Since publishing my first book and taking to social media there have been two words that seem to keep popping up.

Hope and inspiration.

At first I never knew what sort of people were writing the comments. It was nice to read regardless that people valued what I'm trying to achieve. I can now confirm after hundreds, perhaps thousands of direct messages on my social media that the most common is family members of addicts. Of course I can't mention names, everything shared to me in a direct message will always stay confidential.

The stories I've heard have given me a new outlook on what trauma means, horrific stories and these mostly come from family members of addicts, sometimes addicts themselves. I give people hope that their loved ones can one day turn their life around. That to me is priceless and very humbling. Initially, I thought it was all about the addicts, trying to guide and help them. Turns out I have many different groups of people intrigued in my story.

We firstly have the addicts of this world who are looking to genuinely change. They want to stop but just don't know how. Secondly you have family members and friends of addicts who I help by giving hope. Thirdly, there is a group of people with no knowledge of addiction but are negatively judgemental of all addicts and are learning that they are wrong. They are starting to understand that addiction can happen to anyone. That all addicts are human beings and just made bad choices, Therefore changing their mindset with regards to addicts and addiction. Finally, I have a group of people full of hate towards addicts.

Personally I acknowledge and understand each group. Even the haters make valid points. If you or your granny have been robbed at knife point from a heroin addict looking for a fix, of course you're going to have a negative mindset towards all heroin addicts. I will always try to make these sorts of people understand we are all individuals. Some of the nicest, kindest people I've ever met in my life were drug addicts. A mindset is very difficult to change when you believe you're correct and can back it up with your own lived experiences. I'm not stating all drug addicts are nice people. They are not.What I state is there are good people and bad people on this earth regardless of addiction. Good people make bad choices and will pay for their choices their whole lives.

If we don't want addicts in society then we must help them get clean, not spit on them when they are down. We don't know what traumatic lives people have had to make them become an addict. Lots of addicts don't even know why they are addicts because nobody has taken the time to understand. The true reasons are hidden so deep that it's incredibly difficult to ask someone to open up about a life in the past.

We must build trust first and foremost. Only then will you have a chance of hearing the true story of an addict. To give people hope I just need to be me, I speak my truth and sometimes it's not welcomed. However the truth is the truth and for me it must be spoken or written. If all these loved ones of addicts are taking hope from my story then that's a good thing, no, correction, that's a great thing!!

 Another reason to be proud of myself. Sometimes in life hope is all we have. I often explain to addicts who reach out about their mindset. They often tell me their life stories and end it by saying, "I hope I can get clean like you". I always reply the same thing, "you need to change your mindset so that you know you can get clean rather than hope".

 There is a huge difference between hoping and knowing. I know lots of addicts around the world can get clean. They hope they can and often fail. This all comes from self belief. As an addict we are most definitely lacking in self belief. This doesn't mean I'm just trying to educate them. Most addicts don't want to hear anyone talking about how to get clean because they have already accepted their fate. I know this because I have, hence why I won't give up trying to plant seeds.

 Even if I'm reaching just one person it all becomes worth it.

Celebrating 18 years off heroin

HOMELESS

I have been very naive many times in my life. One of the most recent times I can think of was when I was sitting listening to music and finishing my first book. I had this great idea to donate all the profits to homelessness in Scotland.

I genuinely believed that I could start a ball rolling that would bring charities together under one umbrella! I now understand how ludacris a notion that was.

Charities are so self indulged in their own funding that they have lost sight of the bigger picture. It seems to me that they are competing rather than all working together to fix the problems they state in their mission statements. It's very frustrating and makes me angry to find out that this sector is also full of greedy people. Like I said, I've been very naive in my thought process. I felt assured that these military charities would want to help me with my book. It turns out that none of them did, I found this shocking. I've raised over £13,000 so far with the sales of my first book, but imagine what I could have raised if they had helped me promote, ' A conflict of interest one well known Scottish military told me! I never understood what they meant and still dont to be honest. I emailed them all and all I was asking for was to share a pic of my book on their social media. Mention a little bit about me and that all the money goes to homelessness in Scotland.

I've documented where all the money has gone so far so they don't question my integrity. I have travelled all across Scotland on my own handing out military sleeping bags to the homeless, I have donated thousands of pounds to homeless charities all across Scotland. Some of them didn't even say thankyou. Of course I'm not doing it for a thankyou but it shows the sorts of people I'm dealing with.

I had to purchase military sleeping bags from Wales because the military people that I had contacted told me that they wouldn't donate all the bags that are incinerated because if a homeless person is found dead in a military sleeping bag that would look really bad!! I remember having the phone call and I just gasped! This makes no sense to me. I explained that I'd have all the rips repaired before handing them out but they didn't want to hear it. These military sleeping bags are far better than your average civilian sleeping bag and to burn them when they are needed on our streets really just angers me. So homeless people can die, some of which are veterans as long as they're not found in a military sleeping bag. This is something I will keep trying to rectify.

There is a chain of command and I've always respected it but on these occasions I will bypass the monkeys and go straight for the organ grinder.

Surely those in high ranking positions will see that these sleeping bags can still have a use? Rips can be repaired. Stains can be removed. Homeless people can be kept warm!

Trust me folks, I will keep flying solo until I'm heard and supported. I understand lots of people are scamming on the streets which understandably puts people off helping. Let's not forget the genuine people in need though, Everyone deserves a roof over their head, Sleeping bags will never fix the problem but until the government and charity sector get their fingers out I'll keep helping out.

I've started to save for my first container. I have tradesmen willing to help me convert these ship containers into habitable living quarters. The problem I'm having is sourcing land. In time I will create my own village, a safe haven where people can be kept warm, a place where you can get help with your addiction problems if you have them, a place where you rebuild your life. People laugh at me and call it a pipe dream but I can visually see it in my mind.

Rome wasn't built in a day and I've actually got quite good at learning patience. I was naive to think celebrities would help me, I was naive to think charities would help too. Everyday is a school day but for me all that's important is that I follow my dreams.

I will get a huge break sometime.......

Helping the homeless

Flying solo and proudly made over £13,000 for charity

LIVING IN FIFE

I moved to Fife from Edinburgh a few years back. As a city lad I've always been round the hustle and bustle that goes with city living. The reason for the move though was that I wasn't getting peace and it really started to affect my mood. I was living in the same flat that I used to take heroin in. The same flat my daughter stayed in for the first few years of her life and it wasn't easy.

No amount of paint or decoration was going to change that.

My girlfriend, who is now my amazing wife moved in with her daughter Cherise in 2012, I had recently been medically discharged from the Scots Guards and now I was trying to settle back into civilian life. The trouble was I know everyone, I couldn't leave my house without bumping into someone I knew from my past and they were often wasted on something.

If truth be told,I was also an addict but I had convinced myself that my addiction was okay because of my crushed spine. I made the mistake of mentioning I was on codeine and tramadol, soon offers of heroin were dropped into conversations. I knew I never would but they didnt stop asking me.

Polishing my pride and joy would take four hours. I had purchased a black Subaru after leaving the army and spent thousands doing it all up. It was my escape. I was also using my meds as a way of escape too. Going for pointless drives distracted me from the feelings that I was being punished for using heroin. Every morning, I was plagued with the same thoughts. I really did take my medical discharge harder than anyone will ever know. I don't know much about cars but I was slowly learning. Whilst my wife was at work and the bairn at school, I was out of the flat as much as possible. This flat felt a bit like a prison and the walls were closing in when I was alone. Swimming, gym, driving or trips to the beach, anything to get away.

We had often spoken about moving away from Edinburgh but with school and work it only ever went as far as a discussion. One day my settlement finally came through for my injuries. I remember feeling excited because the bar was almost finished at school so perhaps we would finally get away for a fresh start. Stephanie wanted to move too so it was just a case of finding somewhere we liked. That same night we were both on our phones and laptops looking at properties. We had looked all over Scotland but decided on Fife. Close enough for families and friends to visit but far enough away from the hustle and bampots. Everyday there was drama, sirens, fighting, screaming bairns, drug dealing and drunks were a daily occurance and finally I could escape.

The first house we looked at was in Dunfermline. It had an upstairs and downstairs which was the only thing I was really bothered about. The property was on a main street and needed a lot of work; kitchen, bathroom and hallway were like something out of the 80's. We walked back to the car after being shown around and Didn't need to say anything, Steph just said 'oh well there are plenty more to look at'

We drove back over the bridge to Edinburgh, got stuck in traffic again and I knew we would have a better life away from the rat race.

That night we both noticed the same house, It was in Lochgelly, fifty minutes drive. It had an upstairs, three bedrooms, and the most amazing looking oak tree in the garden. I was sold after looking at the pictures. Steph did like it too but a little less enthusiastic than me. We called for a viewing and soon we were heading over the bridge again. As we pulled into the street in my heavily modified Subaru we both laughed at what the neighbours must be thinking. Yobs haha!

Anyway I cut the engine and as we stepped out the car I asked Steph to stop. Just stop and listen. I told her, It was completely silent. I had the biggest grin on my face. We knocked on the door and were offered to look around. I only got into the hallway and living room and asked the lady 'how much to take it off the market'? She laughed and said do you maybe want to look around the rest of the house and maybe speak to your wife? Everyone laughed and I don't think Steph was surprised!

I'm known for jumping in with both feet. I could tell Steph loved it too. Everything was modern and decorated recently, so I literally didn't need anything. I'm in a huge hurry to escape Edinburgh at this point and it maybe showed a little too much. We looked around upstairs then went and had a cup of tea. I was just so excited and to my relief Steph was backing me up. 'I need to speak to my husband tonight she told us' and we left to head back across the bridge, we got stuck in traffic!

That night I placed a bid and kept my fingers crossed, I noticed Steph didn't seem happy coming home that day, She was nervous we would lose out to a higher bid. So when we got the news shortly after that our bid had been accepted it was such a relief. We had a lot to organise but after a short time we were told to go and pick the keys up. It was amazing to be driving over the bridge for the last time. Next time we will be driving home to Fife.

We didn't have all our stuff moved in so we set up camp beds in the living room and used the laptop for a TV, ordered a takeaway and revelled in the silence. Like a kid I ran upstairs shouting to Steph and Cherise, "can you hear me now?" as I jumped from room to room. We were all so happy and excited for this new chapter in our lives. Cherise had college but the train station was only 10 minutes away. There was a local bus that passed our street but it was a cul de sac so no through traffic.

Of course, Cherise had 2 taxi drivers at her disposal so we rarely used the bus. I've still not to this day ever used it.

The first night after dinner we were watching a film and I heard this noise outside. I've always been nosey and jumpy since my drug days. I opened the door to listen and all I could hear was, "BRIAN BRIAN BRIAN", it sounded like a drunk bloke!
I went into Steph and said "oh no", hope it;s not frying pan into the fire' She asked who it was and I just said a drunk guy looking for Brian I think. Steph got up and came outside too. We listened a little closer, It wasn't a drunk looking for Brian it was the Bull in the field over the back of our house!! We laughed hysterically, probably relieved more than anything. This countryside will take some getting used to.

We met the neighbours for the first time and I suppose we were very lucky, I think both myself and Steph realised that in our haste we could have ended up with noisey families on both sides. Fortunately, they were both elderly couples as were most people in the street. They made us feel very welcome and told us a bit about the area. Many people on asking where we were moving often replied 'Oh that Ballingry is a rough area' I just replied that I grew up in Leith so not many rougher areas to live in. Doesn't matter where you live, what matters is your neighbours and we are lucky to have amazing ones. As an "Edinburger" it's great to live in the countryside, Even with all the bulls and cows shouting Brian " every night.

If you're wondering what I'm talking about, say Brian in your lowest, deepest voice as slowly as you can haha.

My pride and joy.

SELF- HELP

I see lots of people spending thousands of pounds to go to rehab, I never did the whole rebab thing and I'm not going to slate it. So many are relapsing and I think I understand why. It's great to get help to break free from your physical addiction.

As I've stated before, addiction is a mental problem and it's my belief that this is what's wrong with individuals who relapse. In this chapter I'll try and explain as best as I can how addicts can best help themselves for free. It's never easy but it is possible. Whether you relate to what I'm stating or not you must understand that someone out there may take it on board so I feel it's necessary. Regardless of who we are, our past, our drug choice or how much money we have the same thing applies.

Acknowledgment of our addiction.

Asking for help is not a weakness of wisdom. I love this statement and it's very true. With self talk we can also ask ourselves for help too. The first step into long term recovery comes from facing our demons. If you keep burying your head in the sand you will eventually suffocate. This requires bravery as you will need to go into dark places, relive memories of a past you'd rather forget, to heal the wounds you must find them. This does not need to be shared with anyone although ild suggest you do. The bad choices you made, the bad things you have done, the bad things that happened to you, traumatic things that you have spent a lifetime trying to bury in the deepest part of your mind.

Learning who you are can set you free. We are here on earth one time, don't think about a life past, think of a future you can have. As an addict I didn't believe I had a future until I learnt who I was and owned up to my mistakes.

I will never know if I made the correct choice separating from my daughter. This was my demon to face and not easy to overcome, I will try my best to explain my thought process at the time. I was a heroin addict who physically fought with my daughter's mum all the time. I couldn't live like that anymore. It was destroying me inside and I chose heroin to help combat that. I chose drugs over my daughter and that is a harsh brutal reality of my life.

I can't change the past.

If I'd known that I'd become suicidal as a result of that choice then maybe I would have thought differently. As they say, hindsight is a great thing though. My daughter would be better off without me as my daily self-talk, long before I understood what self-talk even was. This person in my head who I have daily discussions with can actually be controlled. If I'd known I had all this power then maybe things would have been different.

When the time comes to change you must acknowledge your deepest thoughts, Once you start to do this you can sort through the mess. Life isn't about what mistakes and bad choices were made, life is about now, being here right now and choosing to be a good person. Learning from your mistakes. Lots of people act like they are perfect but trust me nobody is.

We need to make a plan, we need to dream of where we want to be and work extremely hard towards it. Failing along the way is acceptable, as long as we learn from it and dont just give up. Short term, mid term, long term goals can help you to focus. What I will say is dream big! Society will try to bring you down, mostly from people with bigger demons than yours; demons they have no interest in facing.

Disregard the negative energy coming your way!

As an addict this is a difficult concept because we believe we deserve the negativity and hatred coming our way. Well you don't. It's just a test to see how you react. Focusing on ourselves is totally selfish. Sometimes we need to be selfish to heal. It's not about anyone else, it's about us. If we are to become a better person then take the time for yourself and do what needs to be done. Embrace the positive things in life, these you may feel you don't deserve with self sabotage.

Trust me when I say 'you are worth it'.

Small steps lead to a giant stride and as long as you are heading in the right direction don't put too much pressure on yourself. If you slip then get back up, straight away! Don't bother with all the self pity bullshit. If you find yourself wallowing in self pity then you're not doing it right and relapse is inevitable. We are human. We all make mistakes, so what? Acknowledge to yourself you got it wrong, Acknowledge you need to try harder, acknowledge you need to learn what went wrong so you can prevent it happening again.

How do we know if we are acknowledging our short falls? We hold our hands up! Take responsibility. Addiction does have physical elements to it, of course it does. It will take months for your body to adjust. Even after the drugs have left your system completely and you think you're home and dry you will be met with harsh tests.

At times of sadness, anger, anxiety, boredom or loneliness you will face a time when your mind will try to convince you that it's a good idea to relapse. Hence why I'm talking about self talk, acknowledgment, learning who we are, learning it's a choice that we control. You can tell that voice to go and fuck off!! Literally in your own head you tell them to shut up. Use a mirror if need be, but you have to tell them that they control you no longer and never will again. You can make them go away. You have to believe it, you don't want to hope you can change, you want to know you've changed, Your ability to genuinely change comes from within us, from within our own heads, our self talk, our minds.

When you find yourself reading this book and kicking back against what I'm saying, that's your negative self talk having control. What are you waiting on? You may feel like the world has done you a wrong turn and perhaps it has but to achieve happiness the world doesn't care, you must care about yourself. I can hear you self talking now! 'Im a waste of space, I've done too many horrific things, I don't deserve to be happy, My life has been too traumatic to recover!! This is your negative self talk controlling you. Trust me when I say you can change that thought process. Engage with me and learn or if I'm not your cup of tea then seek someone who you can relate to. Keep going until you find them. I promise they are out there.

For me I had to realise that I can't turn the clock back. What I can have control over is what I do from this day forward. I can try to make my daughter proud of me, even if she never is proud of me, I know I'm trying my hardest.

All I keep thinking in my own head is if I was to ask the people who genuinely love me what they want for me, I think I'd get the same answer, 'for me to be happy and be good.' Even loved ones that I've lost would all answer the same. They wouldn't want me wallowing or even grieving. This is how I choose to live my life.

You have to remember lots of people don't want you to get clean! Certainly those you take or took drugs with. The last thing they want is to see you rise up. If you rise up then you are leaving them behind and they won't want that. Expecting it and preparing for it is my advice, I cut all those kinds of people out of my life. They are bitter and jealous of me and I understand why. I wish I could help everyone but the ones least likely to accept my help are the ones who knew me as a smackhead who struggled. It's difficult to change your perceptions of people. Why would they think I've changed when they believe you can't change?

Even after 18 years off heroin I'll still be a heroin addict to some people. It's not about them, it's about me and that was a harsh and difficult lesson to learn. I used to think I had hundreds of friends, I used to think I had a huge family that would support me but the harsh reality is they don't. It took me some time to get to grips with the fact they don't care enough to buy my book or even message to say well done. The problem was prior to launching onto social media I had an expectation of everyone in this bracket. I understand everyone has a life, I understand everyone is having troubles. I understand the topics in which I talk in detail are difficult to understand.

I can only speak for myself and know how I would react if a friend or family member was doing what I'm doing, I'd be proud as punch and would have to tell them so. That's just me. My wife is proud of me and so are my parents so I'll take that and be proud of myself. As I'm writing this I'm fully aware it comes across as quite negative.

It is also the truth so I'm putting it in my second book.

I'm full of negative thoughts on a daily basis. What I don't do anymore is allow them to impact my life like they used to. I'm only human, and I'm certainly not perfect. I have to self talk in a positive way all the time. I have to remind myself of who I am. What my past was, the mistakes I made but most importantly how I overcame my demons, this puts a smile on my face and fills me with a great sense of pride. If ever that's not enough and I still feel low I think about how I donated all of the money from my first book to homelessness in Scotland. Or, if that still isn't enough, what about visiting schools and prisons and using my own money to do so? Or helping everyone I can on social media. I have a whole arsenal of things I can self-talk about to make me feel happier.

We need to use whatever we have to help us when things get difficult in life.

GROWING

If I think back to that day eighteen years ago when I finally knew I would never take heroin again.Something fascinating happened to me, something so strange yet amazing. I found myself in a position of dreaming.

 I knew cold turkey had not even properly started for me but I knew what to expect. I had the usual stomach cramps, the shivers, the restlessness, the vomiting and everything else that goes with it. However this time I knew it was only temporary, I knew that I had to do it one final time. I locked the front door, I had tins of tomato soup and tins of beans at the ready although I knew I wouldn't be needing those for a few days at least. I was used to starving myself so my stomach had shrunk so much that even when I tried to force food down it didn't take much to fill me up.

 Physically I was in shit state, mentally I was having a party in my mind, dreaming of cars, holidays, girlfriends, jobs and all the other things I once believed I'd never have again. It was a very strange feeling this way when I was in such a bad place but it definitely helped my withdrawals. I had left all my drugs on the table to prove a point to myself. Methadone, dihydrocodeine, valium, and cannabis all lay there for over a week. I would rid myself of this addiction and it's not up for discussion. I would constantly self talk. Crazy to think I often had a smile on my face, That's the truth. Cold Turkey is hell so don't get me wrong, however because I knew I wouldn't indulge I was just waiting for the symptoms to pass.

 I remember going out to meet some so called friends a week or so after, I of course was still in this point to prove mindset, I jumped in the back of the car, Out came the bag of heroin, As they began to chase the dragon they kept offering me some, each time i refused i felt stronger. ' Take it mate you look ill, it will make you feel better' they told me. I waited until they had finished it all and I remember getting out of the car and saying ' I told you guys I'm off it' I had the biggest spring in my step as I walked home, probably a cheesy grin too. Each moment from that morning in the mirror all the way through detox was a test.

 My appetite did eventually come back a bit but my sleeping or lack of was causing me to be so restless. I decided to go for a walk around the block. It was probably three o'clock in the morning.. I had an old mp3 player that I was given and it only had Akon on it. It really didn't matter to me, it was all noise to help distract me. On returning I realised that not only was I a bit sweaty and out of breath but my restlessness had disappeared. I jumped into bed and fell asleep pretty quickly.

 The following days became filled with walks but soon I tried a wee jog, when nobody was looking of course. I was soon to find out although I didn't know at the time that a new addiction had begun to manifest. Running had always been something I enjoyed as a young boy. I wasn't the quickest but I had good stamina. I was switching my addiction from heroin to running and like any addiction it started to take over all my thoughts. Arthur Seat, Portobello, Princes Street and Leith all became my daily routes. Shin splints were so painful and I often found myself hobbling in pain, especially up Arthur Seat. The inclines really killed my legs. Only one way to get home though and that was to use my legs. I would start jumping in ice cold baths when I arrived home.

My appetite had exploded too. I never had much money so I used to buy eggs and a big bag of pasta. I had become ravenous and wolfed anything I could regardless of taste. Protein shakes also helped with my recovery.

Running, cycling, swimming, weight lifting, and boxing had all become new addictions and I didnt even know it. I had managed to fill the void with something positive and the world had become my oyster.

Joining the army was never part of the plan and to be honest I had no idea who the Scots Guards were. Toy soldiers was my uneducated guess. I had no idea that they were actually fighting soldiers. I could have easily ended up in any regiment.

I only remember wanting to do something with my life and the army would surely appreciate my new outlook on life and this new fitness addiction.

Passing out at Catterick. More than a "toy soldier"

SELF- BELIEF

I have shared my life past and also my life present with you, I now want to go into a future life. Tomorrow is guaranteed for nobody so all these dreams I'm having are not necessarily going to come true, I can only try my hardest and what more can anyone ask of themselves.

My life will be dedicated to helping the homeless and addicts of this world and how I achieve this is still very much up for discussion. I know I will have to run a gauntlet of nasty, fake and greedy people to reach the ones I want to help. The people are struggling genuinely. This is something that gives me fear. A fear because I've got it wrong so many times in my life and don't want to keep making the same bad judgements,

I often daydream of what I see the future to be like.

An island is something I'll try to achieve in my lifetime. In an ideal world, money would not be the main hurdle to achieving my dreams. If it wasn't I'd buy an island and build a city on one. I've seen some up for sale recently on the west coast of Scotland. Of course they are way out of my reach at the moment, but I believe someone will help me. I don't know who or where they are but I believe they exist.

If you look at what's needed to make it work then you will understand it's a mammoth task, but not an impossible one. Sewage, habitable homes, transport, healthcare including my very own rehab centres, jobs are all things that will be needed. I'm sure I've left a few things out. People are very quick to point out how ridiculous my dreams are. It's okay that people don't share my vision.

After all it is my vision, but I know other human beings will share it. A safe haven is what these broken people need. To get away from society who don't understand them or spit on them.

A place to live and rebuild themselves.

A community full of like minded people who have either been in a dark place or are in one now. Structured a little bit like the military in the sense that you get what you need when you need it. Security would of course be needed so perhaps some sergeant major type characters keeping things running smoothly.

Think of what you want about the army but things run like a well oiled machine for the most part and I'd like to see my island run in a similar way. It wouldn't be a holiday that's for sure. No social media, no phones, no distractions from the main goals. Whether it's just addiction or homelessness or both won't matter. It would be a place to learn who we are and change if need be. Life should be valued in this world.

All lives should be valued, especially addicts.

What I'm describing comes from self belief, I just hope I can see it materialise in my life-time. I often tell addicts to know they can get clean as opposed to hoping and unfortunately I'm only left with hope myself at this time. Hope I can find the people I need, because I believe in my heart that they exist, I will keep searching.

Hope is great but now is better!

I had hoped I'd get help to get clean. When I did I know I'd never touch heroin again, I did something about it. It was a switch in my brain. Perhaps it will be the same for many others one day soon. Transitioning from hoping to knowing is life saving

Sadly, helping most addicts to become clean boils down to money. I need the biggest blank cheque I can get my hands on.

For now I'll just keep chipping away knowing that I'm helping and giving people at least hope, even life changing attitudes for them to do it by themselve. My hope remains.

I'm not special. I just believe I'm destined to do the things I've been doing. I meet criticism for the title of my first book because people see a self appointed title with a hero in it. I'll never be a hero in my own mind. I'm happy for people to think of me as one because it may help them. A hero to me as a kid growing up was a soldier returning from war, It's for that reason the title had come about. This isn't to say that even if I had gone to war and returned I'd be a hero.

We will never know how I'd feel about it. For a lot of years I was looking for external help.

I believed I couldnt be fixed and when I had hit rock bottom and become suicidal I realised that it was going to be luck that could save me. Was I lucky to find Cyrenians and learn about my mind? Or was it destiny? Truth is we will never know.

I do believe in destiny now however. When I realised that I held all the answers internally it actually blew my mind, and still does to this day. I needed a helping hand but ultimately I fixed myself. Hence, my eagerness to get my story out there. My story is bad for business!

Pharmaceutical companies hate everything I stand for. I'm trying to teach people a way to break free and not charge them for the privilege. I am prompted on social media everyday to set up my accounts so people can send money but I've always refrained. Same can be said for paid events.

Some people will not buy what I'm giving away for the simple reason I'm giving it away. If they had paid £10 to watch one of my events then perhaps they are more likely to take on board what I'm saying.

Truth is addicts need to help themselves and most have no interest in listening to the truth. Their escape from reality doesn't allow it. They take drugs to forget, they don't want to listen to positivity or harsh brutal truths about escaping reality. For now these people are lost.

This makes me sad, as we often say, you can lead a horse to water but you can't make them drink.

BACK ACHE

Having this crushed spine has really been testing my patience at times. I find myself getting angry and sad from time to time.

I am at my happiest in the gym and not being able to do what I love is difficult. I found out the hard way that even though I can still do lighter weights or jog I pay for it in the following weeks.

I've developed nerve damage which wasn't really an issue years ago. The dull ache is always there and always will be, but this sharp shooting pain is something else. In my haste to keep fit I bought dumb bells for the garden, pretty dumb move. I am motivated to do the work but when I'm constantly left in excruciating pain afterwards it really isn't worth it. I no longer have the option to go to the doctors for codeine or morphine.

I am growing old gracefully I'm often told but I'm only 43! I say only but that just gave me the fear as I wrote it out! 43!

Where has the time gone? A puff of smoke for many years is the truth. I'm scared to go back and see the spinal specialist. I often have a full blown discussion with him in my own head. Medications and no guarantee of success is what I end up with. From the day I broke my back, I said to him if I can wiggle my toes then just leave me be. He of course told me that there is never a 100 percent success rate, 'I can have you on your feet in two days and I'd say about 70 percent success rate' he told me.

My surname is Boggie so I'll be in the thirty percent I told him. My dad had a simple back operation when I was wee, and he was never the same after it so I always had a fear and the specialist understood my reasoning. I will make you comfortable with pain relief, (that was a lie) and you will need to lie in that bed for four weeks and not move as your back is still very unstable, he told me.

At this point I was getting morphine which is a wonder drug so I quickly weighed up my options. I thought I could do four weeks without drama. I was told if I wasn't so physically fit it could have been a lot worse. I didn't feel lucky or grateful, but I was still expecting to go to Afghanistan with my friends in a few months.

Totally unrealistic of course but in my head i believed it.

After the second night in Newcastle hospital I was told I was no longer allowed morphine! I thought I'd be a self administrator! Probably not a great idea to give Paul free access to morphine they thought. As an ex-heroin addict I totally understood.

This didn't stop me begging though. The nurse came to see me with a little white cup full of tablets. I held my hand out and she tipped them into my hand.
What's this? Where's my morphine? Codeine, ibuprofen, diazepam and one other tablet I can't remember. Are you joking, I asked?

The nurse gave me a stern look and was pretty rude to be honest.

The same nurse was doing the night shifts and I began to actually hate her. You won't be getting any more morphine, she told me. I argued that it was because I used to be a heroin addict. I told her I'm now a Scots Guardsman so give me what I want haha. Did Not go down very well, not well at all!

I took the tablets and I already knew what was going to happen! Tablets need time to get into your system so I had to wait forty-five minutes. I asked every single nurse who passed me. I was in unbearable pain and I used my tongue to let everyone know. They all looked at my chart and told me to wait. I was growing increasingly angry that I was not being heard. I had this little orange button in my left hand.

I pressed that button constantly for weeks.

Apparently it summons a nurse. It worked for two or three days and I swear they turned it off. I was a moaning little bitch for most of my three weeks stay.

I was moved to Edinburgh after a back brace was made as my spine was still unstable. Coughing and sneezing really did cause me the most difficulty. After a few nights in Newcastle I had changed my mind about surgery. I was told I had to wait a few days as the spinal specialist was off. I asked for his mobile number but was told no, I couldn't have it. He finally arrived and asked why I had changed my mind? 'You told me I would be made comfortable with pain relief and I'm far from it, I replied with what seemed like fire coming from my nostrils!

I went on to have a rant about the nurses, some of whom were in ear shot. Was I taking morphine because I used to be a heroin addict? Did he realise I used to take sixteen dihydrocodeine a day, along with 100 mgs of diazepam? Have I built up a tolerance? The tablets are not even taking the edge off.

I told him just how it is. He listened.

"Okay we will double all your meds", he told me. It still didn't make much difference, 5mg of diazepam wore off pretty quickly. So did the 10mg. It was a disaster from start to finish.
I didn't eat for a few days but eventually I decided to try something. One thing diazepam is good for is giving you an appetite. You received a little card with the

daily meals and you had to cross which meals you wanted. I had opted for pea and ham soup. I still wasn't in a great way and I thought soup would be the easiest thing to have… I was wrong!

The nurse pulled out my table and helped me to sit up a bit but I was still pretty much on my back. She put the soup on my table and promptly left. I was determined to get some soup so I took the spoon and tried to get some. I was doing it blind because I couldn't see. I hit the bowl with my hand and it tipped onto my chest. I automatically jumped. It was scolding and I was quickly reminded of how unstable my spine was.

I screamed out and the auld boys who I was chatting with started to shout at the nurse. Too late though, the soup had burnt my chest and I remember the red scold marks. I got a bed change straight away. Green diarrhoea springs to mind. The sheets were covered. I was sulking for a day or two. Refusing to eat but eventually the nurses started to give me a hard time. Have you eaten? Any bowel movement I was asked everyday. I decided to opt for a ham salad sandwich .

What harm could come to me from a ham salad sandwich?

It arrived and I was ready for this now, my belly had been rumbling for days. I opened the sandwich to look and to my surprise and shock it didn't have any ham!In fact it didn't have any salad! It should have been renamed a lettuce sandwich!! I had my suspicions it was done on purpose to pay me back for all my moaning. I never uttered a word to anyone. I ate the whole thing and felt instantly better for it. I realised starving myself wasn't such a good idea.

In my mind I recalled memories from a life past.

When taking tablets on an empty stomach they become stronger. Still don't know if that's even true but it's what I did back in the day. Same with alcohol. Eating is cheating and all that jazz. I stuck to sandwiches and cold meals for the remainder of my time.

Are you eating? Yes. Do you have any bowel movement? No! The nurse seemed concerned. She started to bring me drinks that would apparently aid me but no joy. I was peeing like a racehorse though.

I got these cardboard things in the shape of a clog shoe. I just had to turn on my side and let loose.
If I ran out I'd often have to double up and sometimes I had to cut my pee short in fear of overflowing. I remember my stomach getting really sore and I felt like I needed to push a poo out.

I was so scared my back pain would stop me. I reluctantly pushed the buzzer, I was still in the huff with the nurses. "I think I can do a number two" I told her. She closed the curtains and left, five minutes later returning with the biggest nappy I'd ever seen!!! 'Do you need a hand?" she asked', "erm no, I think I'll manage", I replied.

I had to move for the first time. Actually lift my back up off the bed and slide the nappy under. Peeing was okay because I was just rolling but getting the nappy under wasn't easy. I could hear visitors coming in for the surrounding beds, I just remember having a fear of the nurse pulling the curtain back mid push.

I prepared myself as best I could and began to push a little. Turtle head now we are on our way. The best way to describe what happened next without being too crude is imagine "Mr Whippy" ice cream, imagine chocolate flavour. Imagine that those ice cream pipes were a little clogged with lack of use. Yep you're there! That was me.

I remember shitting myself, excuse the pun, that this huge nappy wasn't going to be big enough and she only left one?!

It showed no signs of stopping after the initial clog was released. It really was heaven on earth. I felt so light. No more stomach pains either, after eleven days I had finally released the toxins. In the same way I always look in the toilet pan after doing a poo. I look at my handy work after finishing. Crazy to think all that had been inside me for so long. Nappy for full to the brim.

I did a good job of cleaning myself and sat with the biggest grin on my face, even the torn faced nurse had a smile. My time in Newcastle wasn't great and I wasn't a very good patient. My custom back brace arrived and I phoned my mum to say I'd be home for Christmas.

They had visited Newcastle but I didn't want them coming down again. The last time was a bit traumatic. They visited on the day the army visited. My mum and dad were concerned about what would happen to me. All I kept asking was, 'are you sending me to Afghanistan sir?"

Which really annoyed my parents I think. I still hadn't grasped the severity of the situation. My body was broken but my mind was still strong. It's never nice to see your parents upset but for me it was their pity in their eyes. It made me realise what had happened to me.

Determination or stubbornness still existed though. I wasn't giving up without a fight. I was shipped to Edinburgh Royal Infirmary just before Christmas. I spoke the whole journey. Luckily patient transport was amazing. I kept asking if I could have a cigarette. Eventually just after Berwick they pulled over in the lay by to let me have one.. I had the biggest head rush and went silent. They seemed concerned because

I had been so talkative. It wore off and I went back to chatting away. I arrived on the ward and it was amazing. Christmas tree and decorations galore. I do love the Geordie accent but it was great to hear the Edinburgh twang again, 'ken wit im saying like?' Haha!

I remember lying in my bed and playing football manager on my laptop. Family and friends had been in to see me so I had all the comforts I was missing. It was late and the guy over from me had a visitor and I remember thinking it was very late for a visit. I heard the unmistakable noise of a kit kat wrapper being opened. I turned my laptop on silent and started to earwake. I began to hear the noise I knew all too well.

They were only bloody chasing the dragon!

Next morning was a bit awkward as I couldn't hold eye contact with him. My dad worked as patient transport so he was in every morning with a piece of paper and took me out for a few cigarettes and a cup of tea. Loads of friends and family visited which was great to see, but all I remember was seeing the pity in their faces . Some took it harder than others, seeing me in such a frail state.

I only had a few days left until I would be let home.

When I was in Newcastle I had threatened to discharge myself a few times and it made my mum really angry. All I wanted was to go home. Being in Edinburgh meant they could visit all the time but I just wanted my own bed. The physio arrived at my bedside and told me that I couldn't be discharged until I could walk up and down stairs. I had not been on my feet yet which seemed to annoy the physio. She told me that I should have at least been standing up for a few minutes everyday.
She asked if I wanted to try standing and I jumped up. Just take your time, she told me. In my haste to get home I wanted to try the stairs now!! She agreed and I stood up.

Legs shaking and my back was agony but I wanted home.

We walked slowly off the ward and along to the stairwell. I stopped a few times to catch my breath but the shaking died down. I climbed six steps using the bannister and the same back down. I was laughing the whole way. Joking about being a soldier and being so fit. She agreed to sign my discharge sheet a couple of days earlier than expected so I was delighted. I slowly walked back to my bed and started to pack.

The physio informed me that I'd need to wait on my meds. I was all for packing and wheeling myself out there and then. The meds took over one day which really pissed me off. Still a day early though, so I phoned a family friend who came to collect me. I was due to get a visit from Stephanie that night.

The same Stephanie who is my amazing wife now.

I dropped a text to say I was getting home. I never told my mum as I wanted to surprise her. We pulled up in the car and I slowly made my way down the path. I opened my mum's front door and my mum was upstairs. 'Who is it she shouted?' It's me, I replied!!

She came storming down those stairs like she was going to attack me haha. 'What the hell are you doing here?' I've been discharged, I replied! She didn't believe me until the family friend entered the house to confirm it was official. My mum gave me the biggest hug she could without hurting me and we had a cuppa.
I was still going to spend a lot of time on my back but at least I was going to be in my own bed. My flatmate had been preparing for my arrival and he was amazing at looking after me. We played so much Call of Duty on the Xbox. He helped with my exercises and did all the shopping. I was so happy to be home. I asked Stephanie if she wanted to visit me. She of course jumped at the chance!

I knew Stephanie from our Safeway days so it wasn't awkward at all. She was soon to be mothering me and taking care of me. I needed a bath and I didn't want my flatmate to help me but Stephanie on the other hand I would happily help. I had four weeks of growth on my face which also needed sorting. I've never been one for facial hair, too itchy for me.

I was always curious about how I would look with a moustache though. There is a picture somewhere but of course I'm not looking very well. Regardless, a moustache is definitely not for me.

Steph really took over caring for me and we became the best of friends. I have a strange sense of humour and Steph always gave me it back. This was a breath of fresh air because most girls I'd spent time with didn't have a sense of humour. It usually ended in a huge argument because I was so cheeky. Life's too short to spend time with miserable people. I need to find someone that enjoys a laugh and I definitely did that when I found Steph.

The fact she is beautiful inside and out is actually just a bonus.

The only problem for me in the early days was that Steph had a young daughter. I often sat worrying about how I would be as a father figure. I had decided I didn't want any more kids after I failed as a father the first time round. This gave me much to think about. I wanted to be with Steph but didn't and couldn't fail again. Cherise was an amazing bubbly kid. She was eight years old. Well mannered too which was one of the deciding factors. I wouldn't be able to handle a spoiled little brat and I knew that. She did of course know how to work her mother as all eight year olds do.

Steph felt guilty for the break up with the bairns dad so gave her everything she wanted. I understood that, but did explain it wouldn't fly with me. I was a strict step-dad and that's what Steph wanted too. Luckily for me Cherise could take a telling and she understood why I was being strict. We grew up in the same area so I often explained the ways of the street to her, things to look out for.

To pass on knowledge was a great feeling. I certainly wasn't failing as a step-dad.

Nothing could make up for my failure as dad but having Cherise in my life certainly went a long way to mending some really deep wounds.

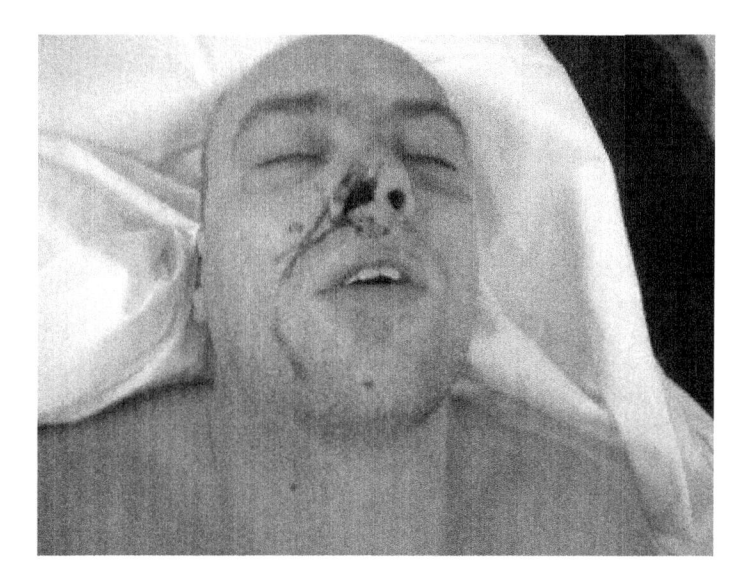

After the car crash.

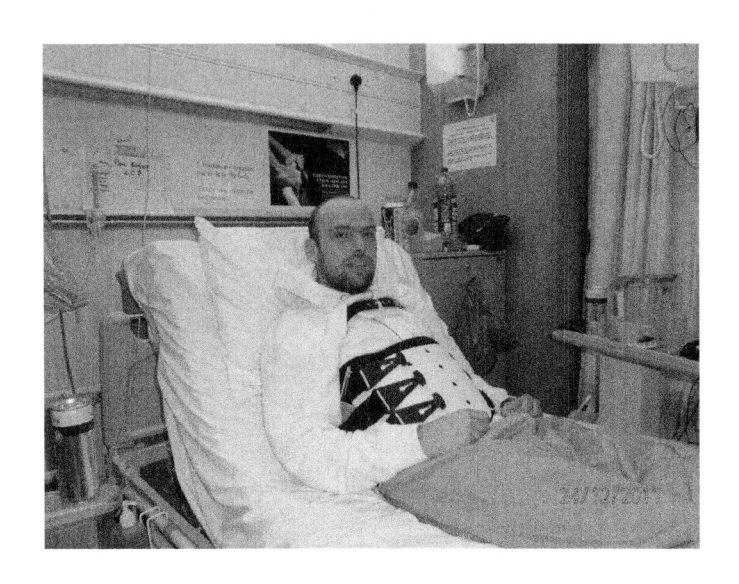

Sitting up with a broken back

Just out of hospital with the facial hair

WRITING

I really enjoy writing, not as much as talking mind you. Writing offers me a way of sharing my thoughts. I love that people who read my words are using their imaginations to visualise in their own heads. I find it therapeutic and calming.

Of course, when I write about certain subjects it takes me back to a place I don't want to visit. This is necessary so that the readers get to know me, warts and all. I feel if I hold back I would become a fraud. I write down what I'd happily say out loud.

This is my new found braveness shining through. I've been a coward for most of my early years so to finally find braveness is a great feeling. To write things down that I know will upset people and make them angry isn't nice. I think if it's true then I shouldn't be scared to say it or write it.

Especially when it comes to drugs and mental health issues.

I was recently asked to write a piece for the Courier. They had helped share my story when I visited HMP Perth and I was honoured to be asked. Drug consumption rooms were the subject. Something I have an opinion on of course. I have just asked permission to add it to the book to let you all read it and they agreed. What I write down or say is just my opinion. I'm open minded enough to be corrected on certain things or even enter into debates.

This is my second book and I don't know if there will be a third. It depends on whether people ask for one. People seem to enjoy my style of writing and I hope whoever is reading this has enjoyed the first book and this one.

Writing books about my life just requires me to sit and remember a life past. I find it very natural but whether it's any good or not will be up for debate I suppose.

I donated all the profits from my first book and if people only bought it for that reason then that's cool. Time will tell if people are actually interested in my life. Enough to buy my second book and potentially more. I need to support my family now and with my injuries I'm so restricted to what I can do. The government deem me able to work and have declined all my PIP applications so I rely on my wife too much at the moment.

Maybe I can continue to be a successful author and continue doing something I love.

One thing for sure is that everything bad in my life doesn't have to go to waste, whether it's writing or talking it really doesn't matter.

Sharing my story can help people not feel so alone. It can also let people see that there is hope. This to me on a personal level is priceless.

It's true what they say, some things money really can't buy.

Cherise with my first book

METHADONE PROGRAMME

This is a subject that really does split opinions. There are no right and wrong answers here.

Everyone has had different experiences and I suppose it's only fair that I share with you why I'm against it. I do however acknowledge the benefits of the program and I'll also share my thoughts on the positives.

Let's start with the positives.

Methadone can relieve a lot of stress on the user. When you come off heroin and go onto methadone you are able to go to a doctor and chemist to take away your pain. There can also be a decrease in drug related crimes. No longer will people need to steal and rob for a fix. Stability is a big issue for an addict and methadone can help stabilise. People can function in society. I'm sure there will be more things I've left out. Like I said though, I'm against the methadone program and I'll share my own experiences with you.

Now onto the negatives from my perspective.

Negatives are methadone is also a poisonous mind altering drug. Jumping out the frying pan to only hit the fire burning below is not a solution. It should only be a temporary fix. Methadone was created for pain relief by the Germans. It certainly does work but like heroin, it's also highly addictive.

When I finally was put on the methadone program I felt relief. I had this green liquid to take away my physical withdrawals. I however still loved heroin. I wasn't able to break free from my best friend yet. I found myself in a sticky situation because as the greedy addict I was I often found myself abusing both drugs at the same time.

I became a bit of a zombie during these times. If I had no money for heroin I would sell my methadone. There was never a shortage of people willing to buy it. Queues of people were always outside waiting on people willing to sell. I would sell my methadone if I was hard up or take both when I was a little more flush.

For me methadone should only be used as a stepping stone. At first I had to go on supervision. I would be put into a small room and the chemist staff would watch me drink it.

Shortly after though I'm given it to take away and that's when the problems arise.

On a Friday I would be given a whole weekend's worth. I would open the bag and guzzle the whole lot down on my walk home. Weekends were a time for heroin anyway or so I used to convince myself. If needed I would buy some.

Methadone rots your skin, bones, teeth and hair.

I held a poll on my social media to see what other peoples thoughts were and the results showed what I already knew, straight down the middle. Just as many for methadone as are against it.

I think the people who are actually on methadone or have been on it opinions matter more. I think the government should be more focused on getting people clean rather than filling pharmaceutical companies pockets and leaving people to literally rot away. Anyway it's just my opinion and because of my lived experience with the drug I feel I'm warranted to have such an opinion. In my opinion, too many people shout about being clean whilst still using methadone.

Methadone is destructive and addictive. Well done for getting off heroin because that in itself is amazing, however you are not clean! Clean from heroin you should be saying.

Many, many people on methadone will be butt hurt and angry when they read this but it's true so I'll state it.

BULLYING

I have had a run in with many bullies in my life. It's a normal part of life at school, it's almost acceptable in some people's eyes. Kids can be cruel and have no problems venting in your direction if you happen to be in the vicinity.

Gangs are by far the worst! It's encouraged just so everyone can have a laugh. I'm sure bullies at school dont think about the trauma caused to the individuals. Adults however have no excuses. At school the only reason I wasn't severely bullied was because of my older brother.

I was bullied on odd occasions but I witnessed some horrific bullying at school.

People being battered for walking down the corridor. I often felt like jumping in but I never did, cowardly I didn't want the spotlight on me. I never participated but does that make it right? Defenceless people being targeted everyday because their parents couldn't afford the best of designer clothes. It often happened when people were trying to be integrated into a group. Batter him/her and we will let you hang-out with us.

If the person being bullied ever fought back they would get jumped after school by everyone. I suffered from little bits of bullying in my early years in the workplace but again I witnessed more to others than ever happened to me. Again, in a cowardly fashion I would never intervene.

All I wanted most of my life was just to fit in. Never rock the boat, I would tell myself.

Things had changed for me when I finally broke free from my drug addictions. I realised how cowardly I'd been in my early life. I was starting to change my outlook on things. I had become happy in my own company and that was an amazing turn around.

Basic training for the army allowed me to correct a few wrongs. There were a few bullies in basic training and I caught them red handed. Rather than being a coward and ignoring it I started stepping in. 'If I ever see you picking on him again or anyone tells me you are, I'm going to start bullying you' I would tell them.

They fancied themselves as fighters or so they thought, until I took my jacket off and walked towards them. I don't know if that was right of me to threaten to become a bully myself but I can tell you it felt great. I realise now I was being a complete vigilante sticking up for the "weaker" ones in the group, now that felt great! No longer will I not speak up for fear of being targeted. The bullying stopped, I can tell you that much. There is lots of bullying in the army but I became a little unstuck when it was coming from people higher up in the chain of command. I always respected the chain of command. Whether I liked them or not.

Bullies exist and bullies are bullies for all different reasons.

Mum & Dad with me after I survived all of the basic training. Delighted to get to passing out day

SOCIAL MEDIA

Having an addictive personality hasn't always been a bad thing. Of course being addicted to heroin is a bad thing.

Being addicted to fitness however is a good thing. Since finishing the first book I've become addicted to social media. This is good and bad but for me it's been totally necessary. Good points are that it has helped me share my story all across the world.

It has allowed me to sell my book worldwide too. During lockdown most people were on social media and it worked in my favour as far as raising awareness is concerned. I wouldn't be where I am now without it, that's for sure. Facebook has been my drug of choice if you like. I've met some lovely people in person and online via video calls.

It's great for me to know my story needs to be shared but without others agreeing and helping I'd be wasting my time. Bad points are trolls. People with too much time on their hands, these people are just sad and lonely and if you give them the time of day and respond you will attract others. I learned this the hard way but now it's water off a duck's back.

Jealousy is a big part of people being negative too. If you're achieving something that others don't believe they can then you will have jealousy. I often refer to Facebook as Fakebook. It's full of people who are not as they try to make out. Running this gauntlet is impossible. My block list is huge. Trolls, Jealous people, greedy people are all on it. Of course lots of people want me to participate in online brothels too.

Trying to sift your way through the good, the bad and the ugly is all part of the journey.

As far as being addicted to social media is concerned I know I can stop anytime I want. I'd happily give my wife my phone and never see it again. I'm not at the stage where I can take my foot off the gas. Arguably, I'll never reach that point. That's okay though, I've had worse addictions.

One thing I know is that if it affects my mental health in such a detrimental way I would step away. Luckily I have a very strong mind and I'm happy to run the gauntlet on a daily basis. I help people with addiction and mental health problems everyday and also sell copies of my book so for now it's all good.

I long for the day when I can help more people break addictions, I have faith my time will come and social media will play a huge part.

I rant all the time on my videos about lack of support from those who claim to support me. Ranting is part of who I am and I'll never apologise for it. I also have a sense of humour but don't really get to show that side of me due to the subjects I cover.

MUSIC

Music has played a huge part in my life. Influencing the way I feel everyday. I often used to hear music and on occasions I still do. Listening to music though is where it's at. Listening to lyrics and relating them to my own life. This has almost cost me my life, most definitely saved my life and influenced me from a happy mood to a bad mood and vice versa.

When I listen to music now that \i used to listen to when I was heavily depressed, I often think no wonder I became suicidal. Be very careful what music you listen to when you're depressed.

Last week I was all stressed out about the Edinburgh Fringe. I became annoyed that more people were not buying tickets. I'd say for about half an hour I was sitting on my chair feeling sorry for myself. Self talk kicked in and I put my phone down,tuck Youtube on and put trance music on. I turned the volume all the way up and instantly began dancing about the living room. Blinds were already closed. Nothing like dancing when nobody is watching haha. I can't go full rave mode anymore but I still have the moves , some people will argue I can't dance and that's okay.

It's about how it makes me feel. I stopped stressing and that's all that matters. I can't sing but that doesn't stop me trying, when I'm on my own of course. Singing is another great escape for me, being careful of the lyrics I'm singing of course.

As I promised , the only time I'll sing live on social media is when I hear back from Michael Stipe in person. A direct message, voice call but ideally a video call. I'd probably just cry anyway.

Music is the most amazing thing in the world, it's so universal. What a way to spread positivity! This is probably why I reach out to musicians more than anyone else. I think one day I should try my hand at writing a song, perhaps with enough editing I could even sing a part. For now I'm happy dancing and singing in my living room with nobody watching. I don't have a favourite genre of music, I know if I like it when I listen.
I played the cornet and trombone when I was in primary school. I actually wasn't bad and if I had been less of a joker in secondary school I perhaps could have made a career from it. I tried drums and saxophone but found them too difficult.

You can't teach an old dog new tricks I hear mentioned a lot. I disagree. One day you may see me on a stage with a musical instrument.

Maybe the triangle or recorder but you never know.

Here I am with my trumpet

PEER SUPPORT

After leaving the army I became a qualified peer support worker. It was a great course to attend. In all honesty I felt I did more teaching than learning.

The people running the course had no lived experience with addiction so they were happy to have me speak for large parts of the course. I finished the course and was pulled into the office to discuss my first client. I was totally shocked when I was told to not share my own personal experience with the heroin addict I was meeting. This made no sense to me but I did understand their reasoning. It would put too much pressure on them I was told. It is a very unique way I stopped but I felt everyone deserves to hear how I did it, especially heroin addicts!

Another problem I faced was when I left the army I was on opiate medications. I was living in denial for the most part. I believed what all the doctors were telling me about me being on drugs for life so I didnt even contemplate stopping or at least trying. This is a huge regret of mine as I'm sure you'll understand, an unachievable dream has been achieved again.

As I sit here in the garden writing this I'm two years and five months clean from meds and cannabis. Truth is I felt like a hypocrite. What right do I have to teach people about stopping drugs when I take them myself?

This thought process ultimately had me pull back from pursuing my career in drug counselling. Lots of people have messaged me to say I would make a really good drug counsellor. I have to say I actually agree but things would need to be done on my own terms.

I feel my unique story can help people so I will never be told not to do it by anyone. I now have my experience from stopping my opiate meds and cannabis to add an alternative so perhaps I'll create my very own rehabilitation centre.

This is another dream of mine so I won't rule it out.

SOMETHING MISSING

One thing I really do miss is physical exercise.

I have spent many years in the gym after my accident but for some reason I stopped four years ago.

I hurt my back really badly whilst bench pressing and I suppose I've had a fear since then. I am very stubborn and although I knew I couldn't lift weights like I used to but it didn't stop me trying.

Being unable to walk as a result makes me extremely angry. It was self-inflicted but I was very bitter at the world back then, so quickly looked for people to blame. I started to experience numbness and pins and needles down my legs. This was all new to me but later found out it was nerve damage. Now I am scared of not being able to walk again so I have become lazy. This makes me feel really sad. I loved physical exercise.

Another fear is that if I try to go back to the gym and start over again I may hurt my back again and end up in hospital. This fear stops me from picking up my dumb bells for long. I don't want to go back on opiate medications or any mind altering drugs.
I know if I end up in excruciating pain I will end up there. With everything I'm doing now I need to stay off drugs for as long as possible. A lifetime in an ideal world but I won't put that pressure on myself.

I refused the operation in hospital all those years ago because I could still use my legs. The spinal surgeon couldn't guarantee me I wouldn't end up in a wheelchair. With my life going the way it was I decided not to risk it. I have met people who have had back surgery and went on to be physically active. I often daydream about what that would be like.

Imagining myself running along the beach again or pounding the heavy punch bag in the gym. I was warned that as I get older my options will be more restricted. I suppose I'm waiting for a miracle procedure. Perhaps one day I will be able to rid myself of this back pain and have one final push at being active.

I mentioned laziness there and just wanted to clarify. I meant physically. Mentally I couldn't be anymore active. I spend every minute of my day dreaming.

Making plans for the future and acknowledging the hurdles I face. How do I overcome the obstacles that stand in my way?

All I need to do is seek out someone with deep pockets who believes in what I'm trying to achieve. Money makes the world go round for everyone in my opinion.

If I had an endless amount of money I know exactly what I'd do. I'd make the world a better place and I'm sure of that. I have it all worked out in my head and one day I will put my business plan to people who have the finances to make my dreams a reality.

MEADOWBANK STADIUM

As a young boy we were very lucky to have Meadowbank stadium on our doorstep. The problem was everything cost money so it wasnt really for us.

Football pitches, outdoor and indoor, badminton courts, gymnasium, canteen, velodrome and much more. It was a huge building which you could easily get lost in. They had a pro-football team which played every Saturday and the Stadium always had a decent crowd.

I believe they are now known as Livingston FC. Back in the day though, they were a much smaller club and we always headed to the stadium to watch the games through the iron fences. It was only a matter of time before someone would attempt to climb the fence. Stewards always had their eyes on us but there were only two or three for the whole pitch. A friend climbed over the fence one saturday and was immediately clocked by the steward who proceeded to shout and storm towards my friend.

Rather than climb back over the fence he started to run away and all the stewards would give chase. This gave all the good climbers an opportunity to jump over whilst the stewards were distracted with my friend. It worked a treat and many of us ran into the crowd. We were not really interested in watching the football to be honest we were just bored. Getting a chase from the stewards and staff at Meadowbank became a weekly occurrence.

They got wise to us so started putting all the stewards at the fence that we were climbing. We were constantly being cheeky to them, occasionally throwing plastic bottles for attention.

We needed a new way in and that's when I had my first experience of a railway track. We found a new way over the railway but it wasn't easy, lots of climbing and bramble bushes which would rip our clothes if we weren't careful.

The railway itself apparently wasn't in use but when I looked at the tracks I noticed the tracks were shiny metal and not rusted. I would be extra careful as we had to walk about half a mile along them. We would put 1p pieces on the tracks and check every time to see if they were still there. We never did find any flattened. We never got our pennies back either so I guess trains were still going along the track.

At the approach to Meadowbank it only had a mesh fence so we ripped a hole in it and clambered under. Meadowbank had a velodrome but it seemed unclimbable.

I'd only seen one on the TV and it looked cool seeing all the bikes going flying round. We passed the velodrome for now.

We were fixated on getting a chase from the staff at meadowbank, They told us we were barred and never getting in. We of course wanted to prove them wrong.
Criminal damage wasn't something we acknowledged as youngsters. We would smash up anything in our way. We had to pass the velodrome and seven outdoor pitches to reach the entrance to the changing rooms.

If we all marched up in our dozens then we drew too much attention. The doors could only be opened from the inside. So someone would be delegated to head over and wait on footballers coming out from the changing rooms and grab the door before it closed. We would all hide until we were signalled. Once inside the stadium the carnage would begin. Meadowbank was full of long corridors, concrete walls with laminate style floors. The ceiling was all those flimsy white tiles which were easily broken. They made such a mess. Truth is none of us cared or thought about the destruction we were causing. The more damage you caused the crazier everyone thought you were and being thought of as crazy is a good thing when you're in a gang, or so we thought.

I was a bit of an arsonist when I was wee but there was nothing to burn. I soon found another thing to amuse myself.

Fire extinguishers!!

Pull the pin, squeeze the trigger and you had the best water pistol ever. Meadowbank was all wooden floors; we could make a slide with a little water.

We would slide all over the indoor football pitches and badminton halls. Soaking wet and friction burns were all too common but great fun. It was only a matter of time before the staff caught up with us. We were in a big gang and they only had a few bodies so they could only catch a couple of us. Being fast and good at climbing came in handy. A willingness to climb places that staff wouldn't follow could save you.

They chucked you out if caught and very occasionally called police but it was a gauntlet worth running for the adrenaline rush. I remember being on an indoor pitch with my extinguisher and a member of staff entered the hall and began to give chase. Their biggest mistake was chasing us, we loved it! It's why we were there. A bunch of little unruly shits looking for attention.
I decided to keep hold of my extinguisher and shout 'come on then catch us you dafty'.

He started to sprint towards us so we bolted out the door and made our way along a long narrow corridor. I was quick on my feet but the extinguisher was heavy and awkward. As soon as I was in the corridor I sprayed a load of water and waited for the member of staff to catch up. Taunting him as he approached. He was running flat out. I held my nerve and didn't move.
He didn't see the water on the floor and went head over tail, landing in a heap on the wet floor.

I found it extremely funny and began laughing so hard. If only the rest could have seen what had happened but we had all split up. He did rise to his feet but was no longer running. He went on the radio and that was my time to get out.

Meadowbank had many fire exits so you didn't need to travel far before finding one to scarper through! Meadowbank was the best playground in the world. If you went into the changing rooms and took a toilet roll and soaked it, it made an amazing splatting noise when thrown at the concrete walls.

In the changing rooms there were always cans of deep heat and deodorant which the footballers foolishly left lying out, I always had a lighter in my pocket. If you take a naked flame and spray onto it you have an amazing flame thrower. I have great memories of Meadowbank.
I'm not proud of the things I have done or was part of. It's just the way things were when I was young. We were just bored, which isn't an excuse, it's the truth. I always wanted to fit in so often participated in doing things I knew were wrong, Things I knew would get me a skelped arse if my parents found out.

One night we decided to try to conquer the velodrome. It was huge and to climb up was no easy task, not only that we had two BMX bikes to lift up. Teamwork makes the dream work and we all worked together to get in.

We tied the BMX bikes up with rope. The best climbers would scale the wall to the top and we would throw the rope until it reached and they caught it. Persistence soon paid off and we all managed to get in. On TV it didn't look that steep but actually in real life it was.

We would sit on our bums and slide down to the bottom. It was pitch black and we didn't have torches. It had a pitch in the centre so we began kicking the ball about in the dark but the grass was littered with shot put holes so wasn't any good. There was a huge hut with big glass windows that we found. It had the biggest electrical cables I'd ever seen.
We soon realised that the cables led to power points in the hut. We all dragged the cables and plugged them into the power points.

BOOM!! The flood lights came on!

I'll never forget how much of a fright we all got. We could now see the whole velodrome. I jumped on a BMX and began trying to cycle the velodrome, I failed as it was so steep. It was great fun though. Kidding on, I was some professional cyclist. They had left javelins and shot puts lying out so we all had a go at being Daley Thompson. Sadly, our fun was short-lived though.

These floodlights had obviously told the whole world we were in there. We would pull the plugs for the floodlights and make them flash. When the police rocked up we would all scarper back the way we came, throwing the BMXs all the way down. across the railway and back to Craigentinny. The police wouldn't follow us onto the railway and we knew that. They also didn't know which part we were climbing up. For those that know the area I'll tell you now.

At the bottom of Smokey Brae in Edinburgh there is a garage which has been there for years. It always has classic cars sitting outside it. That was our way in.
Scaling that wall would take you into the brambles so you needed a stick to prevent getting shredded. Other side of the brambles was the railway track. We were always looking for ways of occupying ourselves.

Craigentiiny had nothing. We had a primary school, castle, park and a graveyard. The graveyard was one of our favourite places to hang out. I must be careful what I write down because my friend Ewan Aitken will buy this book.

Ewan is the big boss at Cyrenians now, the course I attended to fix my life in later years. Back in the day though he was actually the minister of the church. In the summer months he remembers me for being ever present on a Saturday waiting on the wedding poor oots. Basically the best man would gather all the loose change from the guests and toss it up in the air as the bride left. I was poor so I always attended. I loved it! You had to be quick because there were dozens of us all waiting.

Bypassing the one pennies and two pennies and only picking up the silver was my tactic. Fifty pence pieces were few and far between but I did get a few in my time. We would all head into Ali's corner shop and buy our sweets and fizzy juice. Ali had given me a job delivering newspapers so I always behaved because he knew my parents and Ewan.

Ewan also knew my parents so I was always on my best behaviour unlike some friends who would just wait about until the shop was flooded after the poor oot.
They were too cool to get on their hands and knees for loose change. Not too cool to fill their pockets when Ali was busy though.

The graveyard was a place where people were laid to rest but we didn't appreciate that. It was a big playground. I often climbed the roof and jumped all over the gravestones. I would often stop and read the names. Looking for the name Boggie on the headstones. I never did find any.

The school was our main hangout. We hung about with grown men in their twenties so drugs and alcohol were always on the scene. Looking back some of the best laughs we had were when the older guys got drunk or wasted on sniffing the glue. They behaved the craziest of ways and we all found it amusing and encouraged them. The park was where we had our fires, This was my favourite. I would quite happily go off on my own and try to burn the trees or anything I could find.

Bonfires were not just for November in Craigentinny!

Ewan Aitkin from Cyrenians with me and Tony at The Fringe

FIREWORKS

Fireworks were a huge part of my childhood. Most kids would be happy with a water pistol or a sprinkler.

However where we grew up we were all about carnage. Fireworks like alcohol were easy to obtain. If you're ten years old and have people in your gang who are in their early twenties then you can get anything. We also had Asian friends who ran the local corner shops so it was easy.

Bangers were my first real memory of fireworks. Basically they are just little hand held grenades that you toss after lighting and they make a loud bang. They were great fun and we terrorised the community with them.

We terrorised each other too of course. There was always a lot of bullying going on within our gang. If you weren't liked or didn't have any bigger brothers or sisters to stick up for you then you would be sure to get tested. Basically you just had to take it and laugh it off then attention would turn to someone else. If you didn't then bullying would continue.

I had a big brother so I escaped lots of bullying from other gang members. I of course didn't escape the bullying from my big brother. Lots of the older guys felt sorry for me though and this helped me fit in a bit more.

I'm going to tell you a story that still makes me laugh today but it was bullying.

We had a handful of bangers and one of my friends decided it would be a great idea to light one and put it in another friend's hooded top. As the fuse lit it started to spark in my friends hood and we all started laughing, Everyone except my friend of coure. He took one look over his shoulder and saw this banger fizzing in his hoodie. He immediately started to run along the street as fast as he could. We all dropped to the concrete pavement in fits of laughter. 'Why are you running?' we were all shouting. 'Take your hoodie off!' He continued running until after ten seconds the fuse burnt out and exploded in his hoodie.

He wasn't badly injured but his hoodie was a mess.

It was extremely funny to witness but it was bullying. Turns out the same so-called friend would burn my eye with candle wax at T in the Park later in life.
Wanker!

Like most things growing up there is a steady progression. Bangers soon became boring and we were looking for an alternative.

Banshees were next up, slightly more expensive but thanks to our Asian friends we rarely paid full price and often got them for free. Banshees are little rockets that make a whistling noise as they fly with a big bang at the end. They come equipped with a plastic tube that you place the stick from the rocket in. You're supposed to place the plastic tube in the ground to safely let the rocket off. This would only happen a few times until that became boring.

 If you rolled your jumper over your hand and held the plastic tube you could point the firework anywhere you wanted! Your jumper would protect your hand from burning as the rocket would let off a lot of initial sparks as the fuse was lit. These became little weapons for us to attack each other.
 When you are standing in a group of thirty or so friends and you know people have fireworks you always have to be on guard. You can't keep eyes on everyone but there is an unmistakable sound that fireworks let off when the fuse is lit. A fizzing sound means it's time to run and hide. Where you hide is pot luck, a car, wall, bush or a nearby friend it didn't matter as long as you hid.

 When a banshee hit someone it was so funny because it actually follows you like some laser guided missile. The force of trajectory meant it stuck on you regardless of where you moved. You had to make sure you hit it away before the bang went off, usually about five seconds. This became our firework of choice because of the full out wars we could have in the street. A dozen or so on each side with boxes of banshees each. I spend most of my time watching the carnage from underneath a car.

 On reflection that probably wasn't a good idea. If a banshee hit me underneath a car I would surely get injured as I couldn't move. Fortunately that didn't happen.

 The great thing about a banshee was that you could point it and it would head in the general direction you wanted. Someone had a great idea to snap the stick off and see what happens. If you ran and hid before the fuse was lit you were a wimp and potentially got bullied as a result so it was all about holding your nerve. The banshee could go absolutely anywhere. I wanted to hide under a car but decided to stand behind one of my braver friends who wouldn't move.
 The banshee would go in all directions and if it did hit you it rarely stuck for more than a second because of the lack of stick. I definitely wasn't a brave kid.

 One final type of firework I need to mention is a boom tube. These things were crazy. Basically it was a firework that let off three separate bombs, three mini grenades in a tube. These had nothing visually to excite you but designed more for the noise.

Thinking back we were all little terrors and you could easily spot those of us who were actually crazy and those of us who were just along for the ride. My childhood was filled with laughter but usually at others expense. I wasn't a bad lad really, I just got caught up with the wrong crowd on more than one occasion.

If we had social media back then I can imagine what everyone would say about our antics.

We were attacking buses and police cars with fireworks on a regular basis. Boom tubes were the scariest. I'm ashamed to say that I took a boom tube and threw it in a stairwell. Not really thinking about consequences to be honest.
None of us did. This boom tube shook all the windows and the tenants must have got such a fright. I hate that I did that as elderly lived in that block of flats.

Doing things to try to fit in would be my downfall in life. Fireworks to heroin I always felt a need to do what everyone else was doing. A need to be part of the gang. We had many huge bonfires and lots of reckless moments.

Too many to share with you but one memory that will always haunt me was the time we built a bonfire for the fifth of November and a couple of friends turned up with a full fifteen kilogram calor gas bottle. They decided to hide it underneath all the wood. I remember lots of friends disagreeing with them. We had all seen what an empty deodorant could do when put in a fire so to put something like this in a bonfire was a different kind of recklessness.

We built our bonfires in the park next to the primary school in Craigentinny. It's surrounded by flats on all sides. Every year the community would come out to watch our bonfires. This particular year was not filled with the usual excitement. Lots of fights and arguments happened because people would voice their disagreement about the gas bottle. Nobody was allowed to remove it or nobody dared to remove it.

As soon as it got dark we all gathered at the park. Fifty of us congregated around this huge bonfire. Some of us with black eyes and bloodied lips from the earlier disagreement. The people who put the gas bottle in the fire would be the ones to light the fire. Armed with a jerry can of petrol they would walk around the base of the bonfire and soak all the mattresses and pallets. Boxes of matches in hand they proceeded to light the fire.
This was the sign for all the families to come out with their fireworks and have a good time. Arguments were still going on and started to intensify. Perhaps the fire won't be hot enough to ignite the bottle I remember them saying.

The bonfire started to intensify too, we all had to move outside the park as it was so hot. The large majority of us ran around all the families and told them about the gas bottle being in the middle of the fire. As families left we were all standing watching and waiting in anticipation.

As more people arrived we told them about what was in the fire. Some were horrified and some found it funny. Lots of people from different areas travelled to our bonfires because we built the biggest ones. Over one hundred people stood watching the fire. The debate about whether the gas bottle would blow was shortly answered. I've never known such a loud bang. The windows from all the flats shook and you could feel it in your bones. The whole ground shook as the bonfire was thrown all over the park. Fortunately nobody was hurt and that was sheer luck.

 There was to be repercussions for those who put it in there. It wasn't much of a fight is all I can say. Shortly after we saw the blue flashing lights and sirens from the police and fire brigade. We all scattered into the back gardens to hide. Usually we would climb all over the fire engine and fire banshees at the police but this night we just left. I'm glad nobody was seriously hurt.

I have so many stories of things I've participated in that I'm not really proud of.

T IN THE PARK

In 1997, T in the park had moved from Strathclyde park to Balado airfield in Perth and Kinross. I'd never been to a festival before and we had decided we would all go.

I'd recently passed my driving test so I was tasked with being a taxi. I had just turned eighteen. Heroin was barely on the scene.

I don't have too many great memories of the two years we went to T in the Park. I was always a bit of a tight arse and decided I wouldn't buy a ticket. I'd shuttle everyone across and just sneak in. I made a couple of trips back and forth in my new black Ford Escort XR3. My fuel was paid for and I loved driving so didn't mind.
When we entered the site everyone had a wrist band. I of course didn't have one, so straight away felt like a bit of an outcast.

We arrived on Friday night and set up our tents. Everyone was on a high, we took crates of lager and spirits and started to party. Lots of the older guys liked a drink. They were alcoholics but back then I didn't really understand that.

They were just the life and soul of the party. Only this time we were amongst people from all over the world. They just didn't know how to conduct themselves, Stripping off on every occasion to the delight of everyone watching. We were all used to their antics of course. Because everyone had wrist bands they could wander about doing what they wanted. If security saw me I'd be getting tossed out so I stayed at the campsite for the whole weekend. I never used to drink alcohol much but I would have a few lagers.

On Saturday afternoon everyone took off, taking the piss out of me because I didn't have a ticket. I remember the horrible feeling. What about all our stuff? 'It's okay Boggie will look after it' they were told.
One of the older guys who had a wristband took pity on me. He said he would stay behind with me, I felt rotten because he would miss out.

The two of us sat listening to the music in the distance, Cheering and screaming just made me feel sad. My friend said 'let's go for a stroll' . I was worried about leaving the campsite but annoyed he was missing out so I jumped up and followed him. He was old enough to be my dad. He bought us two pints of lager in the plastic cups and had a look around some stalls. I didn't have money but was happy to be experiencing a little bit of it.
He started to walk towards a huge tent and I quickly reminded him I didn't have a wristband. Don't worry you're with me he told me.

I was shitting myself as we got closer to the fluorescent security jackets. 'The laddie has lost his wristband he told them, I dropped my pettied lip as I looked at them and he waved us through. I had the biggest grin on my face which delighted my friend. We entered the tent and I remember the smoke. It was filled with smoke. The crowd were all going crazy and jumping up and down, I'd never seen anything like it. The only concert I'd ever been to was REM at Murrayfield but this was different.

Everyone seemed wasted.

We stood at the back and watched Fran Healy who is the lead singer of Travis jump around on stage. It was such a memorable moment. Fran stopped singing halfway through a song and signalled the security to lift the sides of the huge tent up. It was absolutely pissing down!! He then proceeded to sing, '"Why does it always rain on me", I became a huge Travis fan after that. I couldn't thank my friend enough. We left to go back to the campsite to wait on everyone returning. They were all on cloud nine. "Did you have a good day Boogie?"

Taking the piss of course, I just looked over at my friend and smiled. He smiled back and I just ignored their questioning about what I'd been up to.

That night one of my friends returned with a bag of speed (amphetamine). He was passing it around to everyone. Initially I refused and just stuck with my lager. Later I approached him when nobody was looking and asked if he had any left. He passed me a little plastic bag with some powder in the bottom. I tipped it onto the palm of my hand and licked it all, it tasted disgusting so quickly guzzled some lager down. Nobody would know I'd done it so I wouldn't get grassed to my big brother who would definitely have had something to say when we returned home.

It was our secret.

I told my friend and he agreed. He knew he would get a hard time from my brother too which suited me. Everyone climbed into the biggest tent and we lit tons of candles, played some music and joked about. As everyone was starting to lay down to go to sleep they blew the candles out, but I had just taken speed for the first time so I will be up all night partying! Or so I thought. I took out my lighter and relit the biggest candle. I had heard stories of what speed was like so fully expected to be awake all night. My friends moaned at me for relighting it but I didn't care. They didn't know what I knew. I don't think it was speed because I felt no different and I had fallen asleep!!

First light, I awoke and to my horror I couldn't open my eyes. I sat up and lifted my hand to my face, I felt all the candle wax over my eye. I quickly screamed and jumped out the tent. All the commotion caused others to wake up. I'm blinded and I screamed!

I could tell on everyone's faces was a look of horror which just made me worse. I began freaking out even more. There was a first aid tent and I showed the direction to go. When I arrived there a first aider who saw me approach and she grabbed my arm and led me past everyone queuing up. This made me even worse! I was sure I was going to be blinded and the paramedics didn't help. They seemed genuinely worried.

Eventually they managed to scrape it all away because I had been sleeping at the time my eye was closed which saved me. I returned to my friends, some of which were still laughing. This was standard for our group of friends. I had huge burn marks all across my back too. I had singed my clothes to bare skin. |Three big holes the size of tennis balls. Everyone started to question what had happened and apparently one of my friends had woken up only to be annoyed that I'd relit the candle and fell asleep. He had poured the candle wax all over me.

To this day we will never know but apparently he did confess later.

CHASING THE DRAGON

At first we didn't believe we could become addicted. What does smoking heroin feel like?

I'll try and explain it the best I can for you. We found out after a few months that you can in fact become addicted to heroin by chasing the dragon. Basically you need tin foil to put the powder on. Once you apply heat to the underside of the foil it will liquidise. You take a foil tube and inhale the smoke that leaves the foil as you chase this small blob down the crevice in the foil.

Like most drugs there is a specific feeling that occurs, If it doesn't feel good then you wouldn't continue to use them would you. Physically something happens to the body with all mind altering drugs. If it's cocaine, ecstasy or amphetamine you're likely to want to party and talk. With heroin it's the opposite. They all offer an escape from reality but with heroin you will want to be left alone. Physically you enter into a coma-like state. You are awake but look like you're sleeping.

Unlike injecting it takes a little more time to get your hit when smoking it. On first trying it I felt physically sick and dizzy which I didn't like. It also stunk like rotten fish.

Mentally I was in heaven.

I noticed that it took all my worries away. Past, present and future. It truly was amazing. All the feelings of sickness and dizziness were a small price to pay for being able to forget. This is why I became addicted. It feels nice having no worries at least for a short time. I fully understand why we have heroin issues in this world. We had no education with regards to smoking heroin so naively we believed we would be able to stop whenever we wanted. Many times joking with each other about who was addicted and who wasn't. Sadly those same friends died from their drug abuse in recent years.

Initially you are content with escaping your reality not really thinking about consequences. Everyday meeting up to chase this little brown blob up and down the foil until it disappears. Physically and financially things early on didn't really take its toll.

We all worked full time jobs and things seemed to be going okay. The realisation that we had become addicted shocked most of us. No longer were we joking and laughing about becoming addicted. We had tempted fate and our reality was about to change forever. I believed I had signed my own death warrant. I remember sitting in my car waiting on heroin and realising what I'd done.

I wanted to forget so when heroin arrived we knew we would be able to.

Something happened from that point onwards, It became not so much about the escaping reality and more about not becoming ill.
This is hell on earth.

Fear and anxiety everyday wondering when we would get our next fix. When I speak about heroin being amazing that shocks some people. It's amazing that it offers you escape but my happiest memories are of being on the brink of going cold turkey and finally getting heroin. Those first few lines up and down the foil offering me instant medicine. This is truly amazing and only drug addicts will understand that feeling. Physically and mentally healed in an instant.

My years chasing the dragon meant heroin had become my best friend. Even when I went onto the methadone programme I still missed the tin foil. I didn't need heroin physically but mentally I missed it. I had built up this positive relationship with having a silver foil tube in my mouth. It's sad that some of my happiest memories in life are of taking heroin.

However, if you take heroin everyday you will become addicted. Injecting it, smoking it in a joint, snorting it or chasing the dragon. Being a heroin addict is anything but amazing. It's so destructive. It's destroying families all over the world.

Truth is I believe families suffer more than the addict themselves.

Having no understanding of why your loved one has entered into self destruct mode must be horrific. When all my feelings of guilt and shame plagued my life I had heroin to turn to. What did my mum and dad have?

My selfishness overrode everything.

I would constantly lie about my drug use or my ambitions to get clean. To my parents they could only see the physical side of my addiction. My dad would constantly say 'just stop! Look what it's doing to your mum! This breaks my heart.

As I fight back tears reliving those moments I'm self talking about what I'm doing in life now and how proud they are. This makes me smile. I can never change the past but I have a say in the present and the future.

COURIER

We are facing a crisis in Scotland and until things change we will continue to needlessly lose lives to drugs. Overdose, accidental overdose and suicide all plague our society. And we will never stop all deaths but we can prevent some.

That is why I welcome consultation on the Drug Death Prevention Scotland Bill, which could open the door to consumption rooms in Scotland. Giving addicts a safe place to take drugs is an essential step.

afe consumption rooms could also give the government an opportunity to offer support that is not being provided at present. Meanwhile much more work is also needed to tackle the horrendous stigma attached to addicts greg

As an ex-heroin addict, I know many will avoid consumption rooms out of shame and embarrassment. And who can blame them when society judges them so harshly? On May 14 2022, I hit eighteen years clean off heroin.

I only managed that because I faced my demons and put the work into understanding what was going on in my own mind. If addicts were able to take drugs in a safe environment many more might be able to open up about their struggles while they're there.But they have to understand that these are places where they can go for support without being judged. Education is another crucial part of what is needed to tackle Scotland's drugs death crisis. I never injected heroin, I chased the dragon(smoking with foil) for seven years.

This continued every day until one day I couldn't get the drug.

When cold turkey started to take hold, so did the shocking reality that I was in fact a heroin addict. It's why I believe so strongly in education as part of a package of measures to tackle Scotland's problem with addiction. My education as a youngster involved a picture of a needle, a belt and a spoon. If I had known I could still become a heroin addict through smoking it I might have avoided it.

I do school visits now and I have spoken to many parents, who show justified anxiety about what I'm teaching children. "I don't want my kids hearing about heroin," they tell me. I fully understand this but I always argue that your kids will encounter drugs, regardless of how much you try to protect them when they're small.

Isn't it better to educate them so that they know the dangers? I came from a loving family, a well respected family. When I was actively using drugs I didn't care about what my family thought, or society. Heroin was my best friend and it allowed me to escape all negative emotions about who I had become. I made a bad choice in my naivety and I paid the price, but I'm still one of the very lucky ones. I'm alive, unlike so many of my friends. I'm drug free, unlike most of the friends I used heroin with for all those years.

Addicts have to want to get clean and they also have to believe it's possible. And that's why I've dedicated my life to sharing my story. If I can go on to stand outside Buckingham Palace as a Scots Guardsman after my heroin addiction surely that offers hope and much needed inspiration, not only to addicts but to the families and loved ones, which brings me back to stigma. Most people use drugs to escape reality

It's the same for heroin, cocaine and alcohol, but it's only the heroin users who are deemed scumbags. This has to change. And it's why the authorities need to involve addicts in coming up with solutions. Many addicts will choose to lie and hide from their reality.

I was spat on and I know how it feels to hear: "Go away junkie".

If we want addicts to engage with the resources we offer we have to try to be less judgmental. Consumption rooms are only a small part of what is needed but it's a step in the right direction. We must encourage addicts to engage with the resources we currently offer and look to adding plenty more.

FRINGE IN PERSON

How do I feel about the "Heroin To Hero" show at Edinburgh Fringe? I can't put it into words, for the purposes of writing a book I'd better try!

I've rode many emotional rollercoasters in my life and this is another huge one.

Mostly highs though. Because I didn't attend any rehearsals I found myself extremely anxious on the morning of the first show. I'm triggered by others' emotions whether it be sadness, anger or happiness. Everyone was excited to see the show so I got fed up with that and became very excited too. We had a press day at the venue.

The Army at the Fringe has allowed me to share my story so it was a very militarised environment. Yes sir, Yes mam, only to be told, I can now call them by their first names because I'm no longer serving.

On arrival I was made a cup of tea by a Lt. Colonel. Now that doesn't happen everyday, I was told not to tell everyone in case everyone wanted a cuppa. To be appreciated by the officers was amazing. I've had a fair amount of hate on social media over the past couple of years and lots has come from military personnel so I really did feel great.

The title "Heroin to Hero" really pisses people off and without reading my book they make negative judgements. I totally understand and appreciate why. However you shouldn't judge a book by its cover and this is a perfect example of people doing so. Tony was the main attraction this morning, standing in front of all the cameras posing for pictures. It took the limelight off me so I could enjoy my cup of tea.

I am very rough around the edges when it comes to speaking my mind but I can actually be articulate and proper when I need to be.

Something that I learnt from being a Guardsman.

Guests started to arrive at the venue and my anxiety rose considerably. Things are getting real and we only have an hour to wait until the show starts. Instantly recognised is something I'll need to try to get used to. My wife arrived and I remember feeling very proud, Introducing her to all the officers and guests. We were led to the stage by the officer cadets and I took my seat next to my wife at the far left of the stage.

Tony's friend Chris had been filming for the documentary that day and we agreed to put a camera on me to catch my reaction. As Tony climbed out the sofa theatrically I laughed. The start of the show, this was it! All the hard work came down to this. How I will be portrayed is still very much on my mind.

Everything was going well until Tony mentioned my daughter. I gripped my wifes hand so tight I think I cut the circulation to her arm. She tapped me with her other hand and I released the pressure. Sitting sobbing I soon realised about the camera on my face.

I'm an ugly crier so I fought back showing too much emotion. I thought that was it. The only thing I believed I would get emotional at was the mention of my daughter. I wiped my eyes and started to relax a bit. The show went on and before my face was even dry Tony started to share my story of suicide. I couldn't understand why he was genuinely upset. He is an actor and I wasn't expecting to see genuine raw emotion on his face.

As soon as his eyes teared up that set me off again. REM "everybody hurts" playing in the background. My leg started to move uncontrollably which told everyone who was looking at me that I was crying. I daren't turn around though. Nobody needs to see this blubbering fool's face I thought.

This was very difficult for me, but it is over now. The rest of my story is mostly upbeat and positive. There are lots of funny moments in the play too and it was great to hear everyone laugh. I dont have the same emotional attachment with my car accident as I do with my daughter and suicide so the tears had thankfully dried up. Tony got a standing ovation and that made me extremely happy. The show was absolutely amazing and I realised how good an actor Tony actually is.

The following night would surely be less stressful. The previous night's show hasn't really sunk in. I was still on cloud nine trying to make sense of it all. Truth is as I write this it still hasn't fully sunk in.

On Saturday night's show I sat at the very back of the audience, fully not expecting to show any emotion…how wrong can I be? Same parts made me well up. This was going to be a difficult month.

Sunday night my parents would be in attendance so I fully expected to be crying again. To make my parents proud has always been a lifetime goal, especially since my drug and mental health issues. I made the mistake of turning to my left to witness my mum crying and I wanted to stand up and hug her. Why am I putting my parents through this I thought? Was the book not bad enough?

Instantly I remind myself what the purpose is. To help prevent people struggling, to offer hope, education and inspiration to a world that badly needs it. For this I know my parents are massively proud and this outweighs the emotional struggle of watching the play for all my loved ones.

I had social media friends travel all the way up north from London. That was amazing of them all to do that. It made me realise that all these people that I'm meeting face to face for the first time were becoming my new friends. I badly need new friends, ones that can accept who I am and not be jealous that I'm making something of my life. The negative, struggling Paul Boggie no longer exists but to some that's what they liked about me.

My confidence or ego really annoys most people that knew the old me. Perhaps one day they will buy the book or go and see the play but for me it's too late.

My wife is my best friend.

Even after ten years together we just love each other's company. We laugh everyday and that is massively important. Nobody else would put up with my antics. Dancing round the living room half naked and singing....very badly, cursing and calling her names in jest to get it all back. I am a self confessed lazy arse when I'm in the house too. Putting up with my constant whining. To me that's what a marriage is. We often comment when we go out about how miserable couples look. Life's too short to be stuck to someone because of a bit of paper.

I know I'm a lucky man for sure.

I think my wife is scared of what the future holds with my back. I know she would have no problem pushing my wheelchair around if need be. I also believe that all the attention that has come my way over the past couple of years has caused some fear.

I noticed it on the opening night of the play. When Tony got a standing ovation I think it sunk in. We were taken for a Q&A after the show and after that I thanked everyone and spoke of my life, past, present and future. I also got a very warm round of applause.

People are actually appreciating what I'm doing and things will only go further is a thought that I'm sure we both had. My wife is easily my biggest supporter but I understand her fear, I am scared too. Smile Radio and the amazing Chantal turned up to interview me and Tony. I've spent six months sharing my story on Smile Radio. We did a ten part serial called Hero's Journey. Chantal has been one of my biggest supporters too. To meet someone who has been supporting me in person is amazing.

We are working on setting up our charity and I'm delighted Chantal wants to be part of it. I have trust issues because so many people have been dishonest to me but I'm sure I've found another diamond like my wife and Tony. Where will the show take me and my story? I have no idea.

Feeling extremely proud that my story has reached the world-famous Edinburgh Fringe

Steph & Cherise at The Fringe

A poster designed by the team supporting Tony McGeever who put the play and production together

EDINBURGH FRINGE

Overwhelmed is how I felt when I saw the show for the first time. Deciding not to go to rehearsals or read the script meant I had no idea what I was about to see.

Seeing my life story told on stage was not easy and I ended up completely drained after the month of shows. I cried a lot and won't ever apologise for it. The reasons for me crying were thinking of my daughter who I've let down massively. We are talking now but that feeling of being a deadbeat dad due to my drug use will never disappear. I've spent most of my life feeling guilty but if I allow that to consume me I know I would have been in a dark place. As the lights came up and Tony climbed out the couch I laughed out loud.

It was a very theatrical entrance. I suppose that's the point. Straight away Tony went political and I'm glad. Saying it like it is something I pride myself on doing. Greed is why this world is in such a state. Pharmaceutical companies making billions from people's misery is the truth. Nobody really cares is another truth.

Telling stories of my childhood and young adulthood left me feeling embarrassed but also proud. Pride took over by the end of the show but it really was another emotional rollercoaster. The parts I found hard to watch were not so much the embarrassing moments but the story of how I let my daughter down, which ultimately led to me almost taking my life. Being transported in my mind to a time when I no longer wanted to live is difficult.

I remember it like it was yesterday anyway but to have an actor portraying it on stage is overwhelming. Definitely did not help when my family members were sitting in the audience. I am ashamed of my past life. I can't change that feeling nor do I want to. I've made lots of mistakes that almost cost me dearly. Holding my hands up and being honest is how I cope now, I tell people to own their shit everyday because we cant change the past. I've lived in denial but the truth is I never forgot.

I just used drugs to help me forget.

Tony does an amazing job of playing me, at times too good a job. I remember thinking I would become less emotional as the month goes on, I was wrong. When I saw the emotion in his face it always triggered me. I remember thinking why does he look so upset? He is only acting!

There are many funny parts in the show too. I've decided not to try to describe it as I won't do it justice. I'll write about how it made me feel instead and hopefully if you're reading my book you'll search for the digital copy or go see it in a theatre near you.

Everyone that came to see the play seemed to really enjoy it, even professional harsh critics. My uncle George was there last night and after the show I asked if he enjoyed it. 'I won't lie son, I was a bit dubious'

I instantly thanked him for being so honest. Most people are dubious of me and that's okay. He absolutely loved it and would just say if he never liked it. I know this to be true so that made me really happy. Truth is if people actually went to see the show I think most people would enjoy it.

My mum and dad found it very emotional but in a good way. The show left them feeling even more proud of me. Stories of suicide would be hard for anyone to watch but I am one of the lucky ones.

I feel this everyday. Speaking to people who came to the show about their own stories clarifies how lucky I actually am.

Living back in Edinburgh for a month made me realise how much I don't miss it. Traffic and roadworks are appalling! Tony put me up in some pretty nice hotels and some pretty dismal ones too. Student accommodation was a must due to Edinburgh Fringe being on. Hotels sold out or quadrupled in price. Lack of TV and towels I can handle but the beds were horrific. I have a crushed spine so I really did struggle. The amount of walking played havoc with my back too. I put a brave face on and got on with it.

During the whole month I was left contemplating my life. In the mornings I would go to Mcdonalds for a double sausage and egg mcmuffin and a cup of tea, I would head down to my old jaunt at Portobello Beach.

Sitting in the exact same spot I first tried heroin. What better place to sit and reflect.

Memories of Portobello are not all bad, I spent my early years in recovery never away from that place. Running in boots with my rucksack on along the heavy sand as people lay sunbathing. I felt a million dollars as I realised how fit I was becoming. I remember coming off the sand at the end of the promenade and feeling the speed in my little legs. I had more stamina than speed but I definitely wasn't slow. I prefered running where there was a crowd. It helped spur me on, especially when I saw someone I knew. I didn't just have a point to prove to myself I really enjoyed seeing the doubters' faces too.

I would head up to the venue early and give out fliers most days. Being in amongst the army was a special feeling, calling officers who I would normally have to salute by their first names wasn't easy to get used to. Everyone is a Sir or Ma' am until I'm told otherwise, even as a civilian. It's a sign of respect.

I want to say a massive thank-you to everyone that came to the show. I thought about naming people but don't want to offend anyone that I forgot.

We did have three actors from Eastenders turn up on the third last night. I always said to Tony it would be nice if someone famous would turn up. We often spoke about potential celebrities who knew that we were there in Edinburgh. None of them did turn up.

I was delighted when I saw the actors from Eastenders. A nice wee unexpected surprise. Charlie Brookes is best known for her character "Janine" and, Rose Ayling-Ellis, plays "Frankie Lewis". Rose of course, won the BBC show, "Strictly come Dancing" in 2021.

I really enjoyed my time headlining Army at the Fringe. It was always going to be a bonus because it was never part of my plan. I didn't expect to enjoy it as much as I did. Where the show ends up is anyone's guess but I believe we will tour all over the world with it. When? Most likely it will take longer than I want but I have been learning patience. I have also learned to wait on people walking the walk, most talk the talk and are full of shit. This has been a hard lesson for me to learn but I'm trying to be less gullible and that's all I can do.

When you meet people face to face it's easier to get a read on them but I still make mistakes. Proof is in the pudding for me now. I will nod my head in acknowledgment if you are saying you will help me but until I see you actually helping i'll take everything you say with a pinch of salt.

I want people like Tony in my life, people who have integrity. I will never be able to thank him enough for standing by me. He never once asked me for a penny and that's quite rare in my life.

There's truth in the saying, actions speak louder than words!

Tony McGeever looking dapper in his uniform portraying me.

Me & Tony for a photoshoot at the venue

Eastenders actors, Charlie Brooks, Rose Ayling-Ellis and me.

They actually came to see my show, thanks to Tony McGeever

LIVING IN FEAR

I remember a time of living in fear all too well. I used to sleep with a hammer under my pillow.

Months after splitting from my ex- partner and daughter I became a hermit. Rarely venturing out. My daily walk to Niddrie to get my heroin was the only thing I would really do. I picked up supplies from the shops on the way home. I used to eat lots of plain pasta with tomato ketchup. For dessert I would get my flaming hot Monster Munch and rolls. Teabags, milk and sugar too of course. Then back to my flat in Lochend to take my daily dose of heroin.

I would lock the door but it wasn't too sturdy. Years of kicking the door in because I'd forgotten my keys had taken its toll.

I was due to go and pick up my daughter for one of our weekly excursions and as I was walking along Marionville roundabout to meet her I noticed in the distance that my ex-partner was with another man. She had been asking me for a few weeks if I knew a guy called Trevor (not his real name). He says he is your cousin. I always replied that I didn't have a cousin called Trevor so no! I thought she was just trying to wind me up. We had only just split up and I knew she wanted to get back together.

I had decided it was too toxic a relationship so that was never going to happen. Every week my ex would say she wanted more kids and wanted our daughter to have a brother or sister. She wanted me to be the dad! 'Are you daft?' I would ask. We fight like cat and dog so that won't be happening I told her. Mentioning this guy called Trevor was surely just a ploy to make me jealous.

Turns out he did exist and he was my cousin.

As I approached them I noticed Trevor had my daughter on his shoulders. She was only three years old and always wanted to be carried. My heart just sank. Not because I was jealous but because my daughter would have a new dad soon and this destroyed me inside. I put a brave face on and said hello to my cousin who I hadn't seen since I was a wee boy.

I took my daughter off his shoulders and asked to speak to my ex in private. He started to walk away and I said, 'next time you're bringing our daughter to see me please come alone.' She nodded and left to catch up with Trevor. Me and my daughter went back to the flat and sorted her wee pink bag. I filled it with nappies, Fruitshoots and chocolate. We always shared chocolate. Once I had sorted everything we left to go for the bus. We often just went on bus journeys around Edinburgh. I didn't have much money but was happy to be spending time with my daughter alone.

Arguments started shortly after dropping my daughter off. I was still angry that she had brought my cousin, "We are trying for a baby", she would tell me. I knew she was telling me to provoke me and I couldn't resist reacting. We ended up having a shouting match down the phone and shortly after I received a text message from my cousin.

I WILL BE COMING THRU YOUR DOOR TO FILL YOU IN WITH MY MATES.

I remember feeling scared. I didn't have anyone to turn to really, so I dug out the hammer and other tools. I tried to fix my front door as best as I could but I'm not a joiner. The following few nights I didn't sleep very well. Every time someone came to my gate I jumped out of my skin. It was always my neighbours though.

After a few months I received a message from my ex partner to say that she was pregnant. Threats were still coming in from my cousin too and found it really difficult to cope.

I ended up phoning my big brother to tell him about the threats. I hated asking him to sort my mess out but I had no choice. "He won't be bothering you again", he told me. I felt assured I wouldn't be hearing from him again but I still couldn't shake the fear, because of my lifestyle. I also had a fear about drug dealers coming to my door to steal my cannabis. I was selling cannabis to fund my heroin addiction, the word was beginning to get out. I would have some scary looking dudes tap my door and I didnt like it. They knew I lived alone.

A few months passed and I heard a knock at my door. This wasn't unusual as I had people coming to my door for cannabis all of the time. As I stood up to go and answer it I heard a police radio go off in the stairwell. They didn't kick my door in, so I knew I wasn't getting busted.

I reluctantly answered and they asked if I was Paul. I confirmed I was. They proceeded to tell me that they thought my daughter may be in danger. My cousin had previous convictions for locking previous partners in a house and starving the mum of his kid. The police told me that my ex-partner looks remarkably like his previous partner and they were aware that they had just moved in together with my daughter.

I did check google and right enough there was a story in the local newspaper. I asked what I was to do, they wanted me to attend Haddington Sheriff Court the following week. I agreed and they left. The following week I went to court. I was greeted by social services who explained that threats against my three year old daughter had been made. I didn't know what to say. Your ex-partner and Trevor are here too, they told me and I was filled with rage. We entered a conference room with a huge round table. I was taken in first, sharply told which chair to sit in.

Two police officers sat down on either side of me. I remember asking 'what have I done? "It's for your own protection", I was told. The police seemed very friendly so I relaxed a wee bit. Until my ex-partner and Trevor walked in.. I could feel my heart pounding out of my chest.

My hands started to shake uncontrollably too.

After a few minutes the chair of the meeting began to read out statements that were spoken by my cousin. He had apparently threatened to run my three year old daughter over in his car. As soon as the statement was read Trevor looked at me and stated he would never hurt her. I had to be restrained from jumping the table and was escorted by the police from the meeting. This was a very traumatic moment for me. I cried so much outside the room and social services approached me to try to comfort me. They said they will be keeping a very close eye on my daughter from now on, this did make me feel a little bit better.

I needed heroin.

Of course I couldn't cope with everything, Heroin would help me forget. I had visions of being locked up in prison. I didn't want that so I needed to calm down. I had a few diazepam in my pocket so I swallowed those whilst I waited at the bus stop to travel home.

Things began to get very dark in my mind. I was a dead-beat dad who couldn't protect his own daughter, so I became heavily depressed. I remember crying everyday until I managed to obtain my heroin. I knew I wasn't a bad person but why couldn't I stop taking drugs?

If I was ever going to stop it would be for my daughter; the fact I couldn't after three years confirmed how much of a waste of space I was. This was when dark suicidal thoughts started to happen. I'd never thought about it before. It was a cowardly way out I always thought. I had other cousins who had commited suicide, seeing what it had done to my family. I didn't want to do that to my parents. However, I couldn't shake the daily thought process. I continued fantasising about how calm and peaceful it would be. I'm an Atheist so I often wondered how God would treat me if he turned out to be real.

Would God know that in my heart I'm not an evil person and forgive me for not believing or would I be sent straight to hell? Many months were spent self-talking about my possible outcomes. I believe it just goes black and that is it.

The end.

I had spent lots of time at church as a youngster, so I had heard stories of a possible afterlife. Reincarnation sounded cool. I think I'd want to come back as an eagle in the skies with not a care in the world!

I know how lucky I am to still be alive because, I can remember like it was yesterday how it felt when I decided to end my life. The feeling of excitement was unbelievable. I had been playing around with the idea for months but I now had a plan.

It was no longer a cry for help. I wouldn't need to cut my arms anymore, I wouldn't need to bring anymore shame on my family. I would soon be at peace and a drug overdose seemed the perfect way to go. Everything made sense to me and I began to think about what my suicide note would say. Sorry wasn't going to be good enough but at the same time I didn't want to write down how relieved I was.

I'd just be truthful and perhaps they could forgive me and understand why I did it. My family has been nothing but supportive, it weighed heavy on my mind.

I was due to go and pick my daughter up and my ex-partner never showed up again. So, I stood under the war memorial with the rain pelting down and realised it was a sign. The time had come to end my life. The anger and hatred for this evil world left me. I sat on the bus soaked to my bones and crying my eyes out.

I locked all the doors and closed the blinds. I'm actually sitting with Youtube on as I write this story. I can hear "Everybody Hurts" playing in the background. How very strange. I am going to go back and listen to it again then continue writing. I'll try to explain my emotions about that song, and explain why it's so important to my life.

Okay, I'm back. goosebumps and tears as usual. Basically this song saved my life. Michael Stipe told me to 'hold on'. I feel mixed emotions.

I'm happy that I'm still alive but plagued with sadness of a memory so extreme. It transports me back to that night sitting on the rug in complete darkness. I'll be forever grateful for that song. I struggle to put it into words how emotional it makes me feel so apologies but I'm not going to try going into depth.

One day I will hopefully shake Michael's hand and thank him. .

I share the stories with you to hopefully let you understand why I would never contemplate committing suicide. I don't want to belittle anyone and I certainly don't want any pity. I have had a life-time of people who love me pitying me. You can see it clearly in their eyes.

My daughter will likely read this book at some point and I don't want to make her angry. We are talking now and I want to keep it that way. There are lots of stories about my failures and her mothers' failures, but it's not really about that for me now. I remember a time when I would happily slate her mum but that achieves nothing. I no longer have the same bitterness as I once did.

Life is for living and trying to be happy. The only person I'll ever explain myself to will be my daughter.

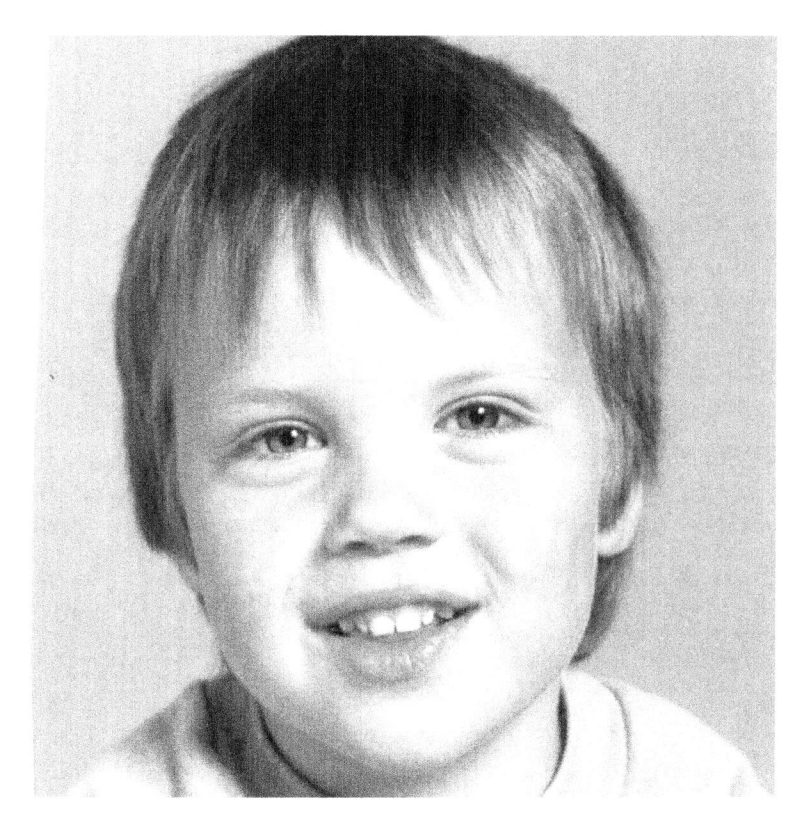

Me at just 4 years old

FAILED INVESTMENTS

I often speak about having trust issues. There is of course a reason behind it.

I've been a gullible fool in my life and even in recent years. When I left the army I was told that I wouldn't be compensated for my injuries. My welfare officer would visit me at my home in Edinburgh, he explained that I should be putting a claim in.

When I put it to my unit they told me no. I was extremely confused and dug a little deeper. My welfare officer explained that when I leave camp on a Friday in civilian clothing I become off duty. When I'm travelling to barracks on a Monday morning in an army uniform I become on duty. As my accident happened on Monday morning in an army uniform I thought I had a claim.

To this day I still don't know the truth.

Even being medically discharged I would not qualify for any substantial payments due to me only serving for five years. My pension will amount to next to nothing too but that's okay. I was approached by one of those people who phoned to ask if I had been in an accident. I'd had lots of similar phone calls over the previous year's "No Win No Fee " solicitors, I generally just hung up on them. "Hello Mr Boggie have you or anyone you know been in a recent accident that wasn't your fault?" . "Funny you should ask because I'm lying in a hospital bed in Newcastle with a broken back and crushed spine", I replied whilst laughing.

You could hear the excitement in their voice as they proceeded to take more details. I hung up not expecting to hear anything back to be honest but the following day a man in a suit stood by my bed with a briefcase. At the end of his visit he offered me £10,000. How the hell can they offer me this I thought? I told him I'd need to think about it but when he left I had lots of time to ponder on the offer. My military career was likely to be over and I didnt even know if I'd walk again.

He returned a few days later and after my refusal to his offer after explaining my reasons why he proceeded to offer me £20,000 like it was nothing. I was totally shocked and a little bit angry. He put pressure on me to settle with that figure but again, I told him I'd need to think about it. He was actually a nice man though, I enjoyed his visits as I was very lonely in hospital. It was the longest four weeks of my life.

He continued to call me on a daily basis and I asked what my options were. He told me if I made a full recovery I would be unlikely to receive that sum.

The alternative was to wait and see what the long term effects of my injuries would be, opening a case against the civilian car insurance company.

I had a decision to make because it was explained that I couldn't claim against the army as well as the insurance company, so I would have to decide. The army had already told me no on several occasions so I didn't take long making my mind up. I wouldn't accept the £20,000 but I would allow the solicitor to fight my case in court if need be.

He seemed very happy with that, explaining what would be involved. After leaving the hospital I had to go to several private healthcare places. They made a diagnosis of my injuries and wrote about the long term implications of my health. As I was an infantry soldier it became clear I would no longer be able to soldier on. I had my whole life mapped out as a Scots Guardsman and it was now going to be taken away. I didn't accept my fate very well. I used Tramadol to help me forget. Swallowing eight in one go to get a little wasted. This became a common occurrence in my life.

I would use the drugs from the doctor to help me forget. I was completely wallowing in self pity and became angry at the world. I was jealous of all my army friends who were able to soldier on. The driver of the car that crashed especially. I saw photos of him on Facebook. He was in Kenya getting his picture taken with cheetahs. Stating that he would soon be getting promoted. That really hurt me.

After many visits to hospitals and spinal specialists we drew closer to a settlement. I had a figure in my head that I would have been happy with but didn't tell anyone but my wife. Eventually I received a phone call from my solicitor who told me another offer had been made. It was more than I was expecting and I just wanted it to be over. My whole life had become stressful because of the unknown. Happy with my settlement I quickly started to plan my future.

My biggest mistake was openly and honestly telling people how much I received. I was quickly taken advantage of because people knew I had money. My love of cars meant I no longer had to make do with my 1.1 Peugeot 206. It had served me well getting me back and forth from Edinburgh to Catterick Garrison every weekend. I wanted something I'd never owned, which was a convertible. I decided on a Volvo C70. It was green too. It was an older car but loved how you just hit a button and the roof came off and folded away. I overspent on the car, I overspent on all the modifications too.

I had never really had money to squander before. Money has always been the root of all evil in my life so I started to waste it. I gave some money to my close family which made me feel really happy.

I've always been a tight arse when it comes to money. I still am to this day. Even when I go shopping for food or clothes I will moan about prices and go without if I feel things are overpriced. Last week for instance I went to get fuel and felt a wee bit hungry. The garage had some lovely chicken salad sandwiches. However they wanted £3 for them. Sorry, but it's too much for me! I looked at alternatives and opted for sausage rolls instead. Two for 99p. If anyone was with me and asked for a chicken salad sandwich I would have bought them and not batted an eyelid.

I loved my Volvo and spent a stupid amount of money modifying it. As a boy racer in my younger years, it didn't really scratch that itch so I started looking for a rally car with more of a pedigree. I decided on a Subaru which I had always loved. My big brother had bought one back in the day when I was on heroin and I was always envious. I was now in a position to get one and decided on a black Blobeye WRX 2003. I travelled to Glasgow to pick it up and I remember driving home feeling like I was eighteen again. Similar to my first time driving the Escort XR3 when I was younger.

After a couple of months the head gasket went whilst travelling on the city bypass. I couldn't believe it. Sitting at the side of the road with steam bellowing out of the engine. Everyone beeping and laughing as they passed. I didn't know anything about engines so I was totally reliant on others to keep me right. This was when I should have kept my big mouth shut about me having money. I ended up taking the car to a Subaru specialist in Edinburgh and decided to put my trust in people that in hindsight I shouldn't have. I wrote a blank cheque to get the car fixed and of course decided to heavily modify it too.

Only after doing my own research did I realise that I was over paying for parts and labour. Hindsight is a wonderful thing of course. I was looking to do something with my life and had money to get me up and running. I was promised by the Subaru garage owner that if I bought equipment I could start up my own car painting business. I would be taught how to do everything correctly. With my gullible nature I jumped in both feet first.

Having no clue of how to paint cars. I spent around seven thousand pounds over the next few weeks and took advice on what machinery to buy. I soon realised that I was not going to be taught anything. I was going to be left with equipment and no idea how to use it. I did try to teach myself but made too many mistakes to mention. Customers were never going to pay for my lame attempts at painting car parts. The industrial equipment was left outside at the garage and the lease was about to be revoked.

I was told to move it or lose it but I had nowhere else for it to go. It ended up being scrapped and the cost only just covered the transportation.

You would think after losing seven thousand pounds I would have learnt. I never did. After many arguments with the Subaru garage owner I decided to move on. One good thing to come from it was my overpriced Subaru which I still have. I love that car but had to recently take it off the road. I can't afford to be reckless with money anymore. It's parked up for now but I look forward to one day being able to afford to get it back on the road.

It makes me feel young and puts a smile on my face. My next mistake was deciding to invest in a tattoo parlour. I got a tattoo from a guy that I served with in the Scots Guards and after speaking with him I offered to invest and go work in Perth with him. I can't tattoo but I'm good with customers so I would be in front of house.

Foolishly I told him that I had money and that's when things started to go wrong. Initially things were good and we had big plans for the future. After transferring five thousand pounds to his wife's personal account things became very strange. They were in receipt of benefits so that's why I had to transfer to his wife's account. I knew he was smoking a lot of cannabis which I didn't mind but before long local businesses started to approach me telling me he was in a lot of debt.

They all knew he was smoking cannabis and he owed a lot of money.

I confronted him about it which did not go down well. Things turned very nasty and my mental health took a knock as a result. I stated that I didn't feel comfortable about all the issues surrounding drug debt. I have been in that world for many years and knew it wouldn't end well. I had made another huge mistake and we parted ways.

I am still waiting for my five thousand pound back.

He told me he would pay me back but he never did. I contacted a small claims court and also citizens advice bureau about how to proceed. Unfortunately because I had transferred the money to his wife and not the business I was going to struggle to get anything back.

I was advised to not pursue it because I would be liable for court costs if I didn't win. The anger I felt was unreal. I didnt want to go to jail but because of my mental state I easily could have done something stupid.

If I didn't have my wife to keep me right I would have committed crimes to recoup my five thousand pounds. Fortunately I never did anything and began on my final mission to help people who actually deserve my help. There are many more instances where people have taken advantage of my kind nature too.

I share the above stories with you to hopefully help you understand why I have issues trusting people. People have been promising things and I believe them. This has left me with many sleepless nights because I'm waiting for everyone to let me down.

Me with my Volvo C70

SOCIETY ANGER

I'm fully aware why society doesn't really support me helping heroin addicts. The way I sometimes speak comes across like I think all heroin addicts are saints.

I know all too well that this is certainly not the case. I could do live videos on social media telling people the horrific things I've witnessed heroin addicts do for money. This isn't going to happen because I'm actually trying to change the stigma attached to heroin addicts.

We are all individuals on this planet and should be judged as such. It's wrong to assume all addicts steal or all addicts are scumbags. You know what they say about assumption? It's the mother of all fuck ups!

When someone has hurt you or your family and it turned out they were a heroin addict, you immediately build a negative relationship with all addicts. This is normal and also understandable. It's the way our minds work.

I challenge this thought process and most people will never want to listen. We have been doing it our whole lives. If every time you went to play badminton as a kid you were bullied or you injured yourself you would build a negative relationship with badminton. Anxiety and fear are not nice things for us to feel so we will try to avoid it.

To challenge society to put themselves in a position that makes them feel angry or anxious is very difficult. It requires an open mind and the majority don't possess one.

We believe what we know to be true as the truth. Having anyone question this will cause anger. What is the truth? A heroin addict robbed your granny at knife point? I actually know people who have done this! Who is to blame? Drugs most definitely change people and perhaps cause them to do things they wouldn't normally do.

Even in my darkest hours I would never have lowered myself to commit such a horrific crime. I also knew many heroin addicts who would never have done those things regardless of how bad things became. Which is why I keep saying it's an individual thing. Drugs play their part but it's my belief that we have good people and bad people.

Good addicts and bad addicts.

Society doesn't believe there is such a thing as a good addict and this is what I want to try to change. I've been far from perfect and I'm not perfect now. I never will be but a line is drawn.

I say work on your mental health issues before or whilst working on your addiction problems. It's the mindset that will cause you not to be a very nice person and justify it. The world does not owe you anything. Even if you have had a traumatic life and you're justified to think it does. This thought process will cause you nothing but pain and last a lifetime. There is no justice in this world folks and it's clear to see.

Please don't wait on that to change because it never will. Focus on what you can do rather than what you can't.

Understand that not all heroin addicts are scumbags, lots are of course. Judge on an individual basis. If everyone did this we would live in a better world. Heroin isn't going anywhere and lots of nice people are just lost. They just need help to get back on track. Help from society.

If you go to see drug counsellors, rehabilitation units or to church they will all show sympathy or empathy with your situation and that makes us feel a little better about things. It all means nothing if whilst you're on your way home you are verbally or physically attacked and called a junkie scumbag, or standing in a queue and overhear people talking and laughing about you.

I experienced this so many times and it really hurt.

DICK DYNAMITE

I was advised to contact a guy called Beans Goldblum on social media about making a film about my life. He appreciated everything I was doing but, unfortunately he was snowed under with his own work.

He was working on a feature film called Dick Dynamite 1944. At first I thought it was pornographic film. Fortunately, it turned out to not be the case. It was a nazi zombie film. After a few phone calls we became friends and he asked if I would like to be an extra in the film. I jumped at the chance because I'd never been on a film set before. It was in Fife so I didn't have far to travel.

At the weekend I was invited to see the premiere of the film at Carnegie Hall in Dunfermline. Me, Steph and Cherise went and really enjoyed it. It was a very strange experience to see myself on a cinema screen. I played a nazi soldier who was shot in the head by a young german boy. It was amazing to be part of it, I've been invited to play a part in the sequel. I was shot in the head so perhaps I'll play a zombie a second time round.

Irvine Welsh and Clive Russell were also in the film.

I have been chasing Irvine to speak to me about my book but still no luck. He knows who I am and messaged me on Twitter. One day perhaps I'll get a chance to speak with him.

Beans, whose real name is Robbie, is a great guy and I am truly grateful he invited me to play a small part. Many people have asked me if I would go into acting. Truth is I wouldn't rule it out. I will try most things once and who knows what the future holds?

I have social media to thank for most of the good things I have going on. I have to keep running the gauntlet in the hope more amazing opportunities will come my way. If people want to be nasty to me on social media then I see it as a test. My reaction and how I deal with negative people is a sign of my strength.

Loved my acting debut - playing a German soldier

A picture from the film

REFLECTION

On reflection as I finish my second book I just want to say thank you for reading it. I enjoy writing because it's very therapeutic to get some things off my chest.

I honestly never saw my life taking such a turn, I knew I was destined for something special but never knew what. Like the time I joined the army, I felt something was missing in my life, a purpose. I believe I've now found my purpose in life and the great thing is that I just have to be myself which is great.

I will continue on my mission to help people and see where I end up. I have to learn to not put so much pressure on myself but, at times, I struggle with that.

What's meant for me won't go by me.

I try to tell myself everyday but I can't sit on my hands waiting on people to support me achieving my dreams. I must strive on and keep the momentum up. I have massively diluted my life story with all the podcasts and media but one day I will be known around the world for the good work I'm doing or die trying.

Tomorrow is not guaranteed for anybody and with my past lifestyle I'm not delusional.

I have shortened my life span for sure. In my recovery though, I am extending my life span. Glass has to be half full instead of half empty otherwise I will be unhappy.

I have a glass and for that I am extremely grateful.

Long after I'm gone my first book will remain for eternity doing good in this world. Perhaps I need to die before it gets the acknowledgment it deserves.

Dont worry though my days of suicidal thoughts are hopefully behind me.

Celebrating 18 years off heroin

FINAL MISSION

As Tony stands on stage just before the curtain comes down he says, 'My name is Paul Boggie and this is my final mission'.

What does he mean?

I am sure there is some confusion about what I do or what I'm about so I'll clarify it here. I just want to help. I don't care if it's homeless people, addicts, people suffering with mental health problems or none of the previous. I want to help anyone I can in life.

People often say to me that I should stick to my lane. I don't have a lane! Of course I understand what they are meaning, however if people in life who I want to help are in the fast lane or perhaps on the hard shoulder how am I supposed to reach them? Certainly not sticking to my lane. It's a fact that so many people have no idea what the mind is or how we use it every second of every day. I want to try to explain it in the way it was explained to me but in an easier way to understand.

No big fancy words that leave people confused. This is my final mission.

I will create an education package to help the only way I know how. Sharing my experiences. Knowledge is king and education is key to helping people make changes in their lives. I'm dedicating my whole life to helping people that society just wish would fuck off. I knew this at the start of my mission and Ive been proven right more times than not.

I have stuck to my guns and continued to do it anyway.

We are all human after all and if truth be told it's pathetic if you don't want people to try to better their lives. They are below you now and that makes you feel special. Some human beings love seeing people in turmoil, you only have to look at social media for my point to be proven. Most people won't accept my help but what about the one person that needs to hear me speak?

Should I forget about them? I won't dignify that with an answer. We all make mistakes, even your perfect pretentious twats out there. I'm often accused of having an ego and it's meant as a negative insult. I want to stay as humble as possible but if me bigging myself up means I have an ego then like everything else I'll own it.

I don't see many other authors donating all profits from their book, do you?

I'm sure lots of authors do great work, people are doing great work for people less fortunate and they also have earned the right to have an ego if they wish.

I often get messages on social media stating that it's not that big a deal! They too have done what I've done. My reply used to be which regiment did you join after your heroin addiction? How much did you raise with your book?

I stopped responding because that's a very egotistical reply. Lots of people have broken addictions and I'm proud of them. I'm sure those genuine nice people are proud of me too because we understand how difficult it is to actually do.

As amazing as it is, I didn't just break my opiate addictions twice. I joined the army, wrote a book and gave all the money away to charity. I volunteered my own time at my own expense to travel across Scotland helping the homeless with sleeping bags and supplies. I visited schools and prisons to try to help and educate.

How about that for an egotistical statement!

I deserve a lot more support than I've received so far, at least that's my opinion! It's not seen as cool to support me at the moment from many people, especially the famous, but I will definitely change that.

GOODBYE

I wrote at the end of my first book about writing the word "goodbye"" and being thankful it wasnt a suicide note. I have the same feeling now. I am grateful to be alive.

I am happy, I am proud. I wish everyone well and please remember, asking for help is not a weakness, it's wisdom. Whatever you're doing in life right now, if you want to change then you can.

We are here once, we are here for only a very short time.

Follow your dreams and be the best person you can be. Looking back on life, be proud that you tried to do good. Failure is just part of it. The thing that matters is how we get back up after being knocked down.

I will keep trying to do good and no doubt make plenty more mistakes in life.

Integrity is a big part of my life. I've often been too honest for my own good and been punished as a result. One time that I can remember when I wasn't punished was when I told the army doctors about my addiction problems. If I had lied I certainly would have still got into the army but I would have had to live a lie.

One thing is for certain for everyone and that is we all shall die.

I now feel that whenever my time comes I'll die proud.

I tried my very best and that's good enough for me.

Windsor Castle

Presenting arms at St James palace

Me and my brothers

Proud Dad with his boys

RAVING REVIEW FROM THE EDINBURGH FRINGE

There are many rags-to-riches stories around but probably not another that follows a young heroin addict's journey from death's door to the gates of Buckingham Palace.

Heroin to Hero is a solo performance by *Tony McGeever* who has taken Paul Boggie's acclaimed autobiography of the same name and turned it into a confessional play. The story is told in chronological order, making it easy to follow and in so doing sequences the highs and lows of his life. Growing up on the Craigentinny estate in Edinburgh he was introduced to heroin at the age of 18. He held down his job for a while but the drug increasingly took over his life, drained his bank account, caused massive weight loss and destroyed his self-esteem. The only thing that went up with the heroin was his level of debt. One day it all changed when he discovered the Cyrenians charity who, after thirteen attempts to quit, finally put him on the path to recovery. With their help he physically and mentally confronted himself. With his nose to the bedroom mirror he said, "Don't ever ask for heroin again because you're not getting it". Aged 30 he managed to join the Scots guards and secure his future.

McGeever relates all of this and many more events and incidents in Boggie's life. Much of it is straightforward narrative, but the Dundee Rep and National Theatre actor turns it into a tale packed with emotional vigour, capturing the distress and discomfort of not just taking heroin but of tearing your family apart, of losing out on life and betraying those you love. But it is matched with the exuberance and sense of well-being that comes with reconciliation and the triumph of having overcome tragedy. Both extremes are captivating in his portrayal of what Boggie experienced.

The only things that perhaps detract are the cluttered stage and an overly zealous sound and lighting plot, that goes to excess in an attempt to highlight and support the script and performance.

That aside it's a moving piece of theatre that serves not only to entertain but also contributes to saving lives through Boggie's commitment to work in prisons and schools in the belief that if he can do it, so can others.

By Richard Beck @realRichardBeck

www.broadwaybaby.com

If Aldi did "Still Game"

SHARING THE LOVE

"As parents of a former Heroin addict it was not an easy journey for us as a family. Hard and stressful times with constant worry of what the outcome would be. We supported Paul all the way but only he could do it and had to be strong. From coming off heroin to joining the army was not an easy task for him. His goal was to make us proud and boy did he succeed. He went above and beyond that goal and has excelled in everything he went out to achieve. We are so proud to call Paul Boggie our son" ❤❤

Mum and Dad
Lynn and Ian Boggie

"It feels like a million years ago I first met Paul Boggie when I was fifteen working in Safeway together. Addiction had already caught hold of him but fast forward thirteen years and thankfully through Facebook we re-connected. What Paul had gone through in those thirteen years I can't come to even imagine....heroin addiction, battling to get clean to achieving that goal and joining The Scot's Guards to the unimaginable and breaking his back. That's where our story and family began, from the beginning I could see Paul's determination to overcome life's obstacles but never more so than the last two years. To say I'm proud of the man I married doesn't even come close. I'm honoured to be on this journey and share the highs and lows together. I cannot wait to see what the future holds and the good Paul will do. Until then I will go on loving and looking after Paul in the best way I can, because soulmates don't come around that often in life."

Wife and soulmate
Stephanie Boggie

"Final Mission - Heroin to Hero, is another brutal forthright book from Paul Boggie. There's no stone unturned when it comes to feeling the turbulent rollercoaster he has experienced. This book offers insight, honesty, raw emotion, understanding and hopefully inspiration to everyone reading, regardless of where you are in life. I have read the book many times over, crying, laughing and feeling extremely uncomfortable at times. Paul's story, passion, drive and determination to make change is incredible. I have made a new friend for life."

Coach and editor
Hayley Tennant